Praise For The Author

As the eldest of Susanna's children, I have experienced her parental rollercoaster ride with a view from the front carriage. I have been an active participant in many of the ups and downs. As a child I never doubted the love or value that my parents displayed for me, though I did have serious doubts about their wisdom and methods at times – as a teenager I already had much more wisdom than my parents! Over the last 18 years on my own parental rollercoaster I have come to deeply appreciate and implement many of the methods and practices outlined in this book.

I believe that the proof of the pudding is in the eating. Although I understand that I am biased, I believe that the wisdom and practices in this book truly work, as is demonstrated in the healthy, vibrant family Susanna has created. Not only do my siblings and I choose to work together in our family business, but more often than not we all come together for family dinner night on Mondays at my parents' home and go on an annual combined family holiday. As a family of 22 members we have our challenges, but in large part thanks to my parents' wisdom and support, we have tried to embrace these challenges, processing them as healthily as we can and enjoying the rollercoaster ride that is being a thriving family.

I hope this book is a tool that empowers you to enjoy your own parenting journey.

– Ben Bateman (consultant to Little Miracles – People and Culture; Susanna and Rob's eldest son and father of three children).

This is a book about what it means to believe in people from their first breath through to their last. The stories in this book have blown me away, they are relevant, meaningful and have a strong message masterfully weaved within each page. Susanna's understanding of value, cultivating a culture of honour and believing in the human potential is captivating. She writes from a place of knowing, understanding and she shares openly from her own lived generational experience as well as drawing on the wisdom of others. We need this kind of loving kindness breathed into the human soul and condition; loving kindness that helps each one of us see the greatness we hold within ourselves so that we too can share with the world around us. Thank you for writing this book Susanna and encouraging us to live beyond.

– Susan Sohn (author, life coach, and mum to two children).

I loved this book and could not put it down. In a world where I feel like it is always our parenting failures that are pointed out, it was so refreshing to read Susanna's experiences and her perspective on parenting. I have many books on parenting sitting on my bookshelf half-read as I found that they pointed out all the ways I am failing. This book is a gift to all parents as it gives practical and easy to implement ideas on how to enjoy parenting. And you don't need a lot of money to do it! I love how the book begins with our identity and how that influences how we parent. It made me think about the influence I have on my children as well as their friends that I have contact with and how I can encourage them and speak life into their precious little souls. I really loved the family code of conduct and found the questions a really great starting point to open family conversations.

– Sarah Steventon (homemaker and mother of three primary aged children).

This book is incredibly practical, heart-warming and honest. The array of ideas that I have taken from it and applied to my own family have been helpful and I have already seen a difference in the relationship with my children. Susanna is a generous person – with her words, encouragement and care for others. She genuinely champions people and speaks life over them and isn't afraid to say what she thinks but does it in a gracious and loving way. I believe anyone who reads this book will see their family thrive – emotionally, spiritually, relationally and in the process will have a lot of fun together and create lasting memories.
– Jo Whitehead (nutritionist and mum to three young children).

As a parent of three daughters, and now a grandparent of five, I SO appreciate the value of a book written to encourage and equip us in what I would consider the greatest role of our lives.

For those of us entrusted with the gift of raising children, whether they are ours by birth or we have walked into this role another way, I understand the thrill of all the dreams and hopes we have for these little people. I also remember the early days and the feeling of being absolutely overwhelmed with the weight of responsibility.

Susanna's book talks to all the things that are important to my husband and I such as understanding our children as individuals and not just 'our children', looking at each of their unique gifting and talents, the culture of our home and how it affects each of us on the journey. These topics and many more will truly bless you as you delve into each page.

I know that you will enjoy my friend Susanna's wisdom, and her sense of humour along the way.

From my heart to yours today I would say 'be kind to yourself'. We need each other on this journey of parenting so let's cheer each other on as we do our best to raise children who will fulfil God's purposes for their precious lives.
– Darlene Zschech (pastor, Hope Unlimited Church).

A
Childcare Expert's
Guide to Enjoying Your Parenting

GLOBAL
PUBLISHING
G R O U P

Global Publishing Group
Australia • New Zealand • Singapore • America • London

A
Childcare Expert's
Guide to Enjoying Your Parenting

Stop Trying to be Perfect and Embrace the Rollercoaster Ride

Susanna Bateman
Owner and Operator of Award-winning Childcare Centers.

First Edition 2019

National Library of Australia
Cataloguing-in-Publication entry:

A Childcare Experts Guide Enjoy your Parenting. Stop trying to be perfect and enjoy the rollercoaster ride - Susanna Bateman

1st ed.
ISBN: 978-1-925288-91-9 (pbk.)

A catalogue record for this book is available from the National Library of Australia

Published by Global Publishing Group
PO Box 517 Mt Evelyn, Victoria 3796 Australia
Email Info@GlobalPublishingGroup.com.au

For further information about orders:
Phone: +61 3 9739 4686 or Fax +61 3 8648 6871

I dedicate this book to my precious family; to each of my children and their spouses who are all raising my grandchildren to be the champions they are designed to be.

Acknowledgements

Firstly, thank you to my husband Rob who pushed me outside of my comfort zone and believed in me. Without your push I would still be thinking about writing this book.

Thank you to my four amazing children who have all added so much to my life and who have been so gracious in understanding. I am far from the perfect mother and yet they still believe in me and inspire me.

Thank you to my friends Darlene Zschech and Susan Sohn who encouraged me and inspired me on to put this book together so others can be encouraged on the journey of parenthood.

Thank you, Bev Bekker, for helping to organise the book, being so patient with me through the process, for all the laughs we have had on the way and for being such a blessing to me.

Susanna Bateman

Bonus Offers

We can't give you everything you need to know
about parenting in one small book.

So we've created a very special website with
extra goodies, just for you.

To gain instant access to these **FREE** resources, simply
visit this website:

www.LittleMiracles.com.au
Click on 'Susanna's Book Bonus Offers'

Contents

Foreword

Enjoy your Parenting: A Childcare Expert's Guide, is written by Susanna Bateman from her unique experiences as owner, with her husband Rob, of ten childcare centres, mother of four children, grandmother of twelve (last count) and friend to many parents.

"The most important work you and I will ever do will be within the walls of our own homes." – Harold B Lee.

She has travelled to many parts of the world, especially to developing countries to coach, train and support parents in raising their children. Sue says in her Introduction, "Raising children is one of the most challenging, yet rewarding lifetime roles we will ever undertake. Fulfilling this task well takes a great deal of time, patience and effort."

Almost all other major lifetime roles we take on are thoroughly trained and coached, yet this rarely is the case when raising our children.

I believe this book, written from Susanna's heart, provides parents of young children a path to follow which will lead to the most gratifying outcome of happy, healthy and wonderfully independent children.

"To be in your children's memories, be part of their lives today."
–Unknown.
Congratulations Susanna.

I recommend this book to all parents and would be parents.
– Ken A Jolly. AM, FAICD.
Chair Central Coast Grammar School and past Chair, Scholastic International.

Introducing Susanna

Dearest Reader,

I am so excited you have found yourself with this book in your hand. I had you in mind when I wrote it from my heart to yours.

My name is Susanna and my husband Rob and I have raised four fabulous children, we are blessed with twelve adorable grandchildren and we are the co-founders of Little Miracles Long Daycare/Preschools.

As I have come alongside so many wonderful young parents on this journey of life, I have discovered that many may have been robbed of the joy that is rightfully theirs in raising their precious children. This spurred me on to write a book that would empower you all to relax and encourage you to not fall under the pressure of being the PERFECT parent. Instead I will share with you some gold I have learnt and put into practice over many years now that has given myself, my children and my grandchildren the freedom to enjoy the rollercoaster ride of life together.

So, I invite you to take a deep breath, make yourself a coffee or whatever works for you and let's go on this adventure of enjoying parenting together.

Introduction

Raising children is one of the most challenging, yet rewarding, jobs we will ever undertake. Doing it well takes time, patience and a great deal of effort.

Some days are more challenging than others, but trust me, the rewards are there and you will reap them. Sometimes the reward for your hard work will come at a time that will totally surprise you. You may hear your child speak in a way that you didn't even know you had taught them. They 'caught' something just by watching you. Children are great examples of 'Monkey See, Monkey Do'. They are watching you and absorbing all you do and say. You, the parents, are their greatest influencers at the moment. What an honour to influence a young life that is so dependent on you.

Funny that I refer to them being dependent whilst this book is to give you tips on how to raise *in*dependent children.

Why is this important and why are the 'dependent years' important?

The time spent with your children from birth through the toddler years (the terrific twos, we like to call it), then through primary school and eventually the teen years has a lot to do with teaching them and showing them how to be independent. As parents, the thought of our little ones going out into the big world frightens us. That first day when they walk through the doors of 'big school' as they start kindy, can bring us to tears. Then the day they ask us if they can 'take the bus' rather than have us drive them to school can have the same effect.

These conversations alone can bring many to shed a tear or even be gripped by fear of the 'unknown'.

How do we travel through those conversations with strength, with our heads held high and with dry eyes? We do this by teaching our children to be independent of us. We use all the tips and knowledge at our disposal to equip them with tools to travel from classroom to classroom, bus to bus and beyond.

Our hope and expectation is that as you read this book you will find tips to help your children grow independent of you, but not only that – we hope that you will 'catch' the joy we have had parenting our four children and be encouraged in this most challenging undertaking.

Value

> It was my father who taught me to value myself. He told me that I was uncommonly beautiful and that I was the most precious thing in his life. –
>
> **Dawn French**

The Value Of Value

This is something I believe in wholeheartedly.

The children in our care must know how valued they are and how important they are.

Everything we say and do needs to communicate to our children that they are here for a reason and that they are precious in our sight. Not only do we want them to know this, our hope is that they understand the truth of this.

Having said this, I realise that many people don't understand what value means with regards to placing value on a person. We understand the value of 'things'; we understand the value of our home or our car because there is a dollar sign attached to it. In each case there is a monthly bill that reminds us how valuable each 'thing' is.

When it comes to valuing people, sadly, there have been so many wrong messages sent and received. The media is one example (the constant comparison in magazine advertising, etc.), or perhaps even words that have been spoken to you and about you. Sometimes our understanding of personal value can be determined by outside influences and those influences are, in most cases, not accurate.

Value means: worth, merit or importance.

When we value ourselves and other people, we are placing importance and worth on who they are regardless of circumstance, situation, age, gender or anything else. We are simply honouring the core of who they are – a person who has been planned on purpose for this time in history. I find that exciting!

We can only truly value another person when we first value ourselves. This I know to be true in my own life. I think of 'Love your neighbour as you love yourself', which we've all heard before. This begs the question: 'How will I ever love my neighbour if I don't love myself?'

I hope I can help you with this.

First you can value yourself by placing importance on YOU and by understanding that you are here for a reason, that you aren't a mistake. Your life has significance.

Today I am telling you that you matter and I want you to understand your value.

I want to encourage you to start speaking healthy words over yourself. When you find yourself standing in line at the shops, gazing at a magazine cover, possibly comparing yourself… STOP… and remind yourself that you are gorgeous, that you are a strong force, that you were chosen for such a time as this and that you have a part to play in the world. You are someone's mother or father and they too need you to be strong and courageous and to walk confidently in your shoes; in your skin.

I'm reminded of this beautiful quote by Marianne Williamson:

> Our deepest fear is not that we are inadequate. Our deepest fear is that we are powerful beyond measure. It is our light, not our darkness that most frightens us. We ask ourselves, 'Who am I to be brilliant, gorgeous, talented, fabulous?' Actually, who are you not to be? You are a child of God. Your playing small does not serve the world. There is nothing enlightened about shrinking so that other people won't feel insecure around you. We are all meant to shine, as children do. We were born to make manifest the glory of God that is within us. It's not just in some of us; it's in everyone. And as we let our own light shine, we unconsciously give other people permission to do the same. As we are liberated from our own fear, our presence automatically liberates others.

Today I want to encourage you to shine, to stand strong and to stand in the beauty of who you are. Let these words echo in the recesses of your mind as you go about your business in the days ahead and as the words echo, let them become thoughts that captivate you. As they captivate you, you will begin to shine and

as you shine, you will liberate those around you.

Imagine a world in which we place value on ourselves and so are able to place value on one another. What a strong platform to base our parenting on. This one thing will bring joy to your parenting and set your children up for an abundant life.

The Importance Of Parents Loving And Valuing Each Other

Our children receive so much of their self-esteem and value directly from us as parents and especially from the strength of our relationship. The foundation we lay for our children through our relationship with each other as their parents is priceless;

> *the power that lies within this relationship is often not realised.*

Children receive so much security within themselves when the ones they love and trust the most in the world treat one another with love and respect.

Our conversations, the content, the attitude and the intent behind them either speak life or death into our partner and into the little hearts and spirits that are always listening to and watching us. Remember that our children are like little sponges; they are moulded and created not only physically by us, but also emotionally, intellectually and spiritually in those formative years and beyond.

As parents we need to be creating an environment that will create strong, confident children and, yes, us believing in them is a huge part of that, however, us believing in our spouses and partners is just as necessary for our children of all ages to feel confident, secure and happy.

When our children observe us building each other up, championing each other and genuinely loving and supporting each other, they feel loved themselves as well as confident and secure.

We have all seen and heard of families where the parents argue often, devaluing each other and treating each other with disrespect and unfortunately, we have seen those children display negative behaviours as a result. Children need to have no doubt that mum and dad value and respect each other. By this I don't mean that they need to have parents who never disagree with each other; the fact that we have two adults sharing life together means there will be disagreements at times, it is only natural and very normal. The very important thing is not whether we disagree, but how we approach and handle our disagreements. Do we do it constructively or destructively – with love and respect or with anger and impatience?

> *The very important thing is not whether we disagree,*
> *but how we approach and handle our disagreements.*

Disagreements between mum and dad handled well can be a huge part of building a child's confidence because they can learn firsthand from us how to handle conflict well. When conflict is handled badly it can shatter confidence in our children. Are we teaching our children to yell and scream when things don't go their way; are we teaching them to nag or to sulk or to storm off and not talk things through when conflict arises? What are our children learning from us when they observe us, their parents, in the middle of conflict?

Hopefully they see us listening to our partner's concerns, respecting the fact that they will, at times, have a different view point to ours, but seeing us still valuing our spouse's views as we talk things through and find common ground as we work towards a resolution. They also need to see us deliberately adding value to each other, hear us speaking highly of each other regularly and enjoying each other's company.

If possible, it's great to have weekends away together without the children from time to time and tell the children how excited you are to just spend time together. Go on date nights and get a sitter every now and then. Again, tell the children what you are doing and how much you are looking forward to it. Your children will feel confident and secure in their world when they see you enjoying each other.

They will learn that it is normal and healthy for people to have conflict at times and yet still have a strong, loving relationship that will stand the test of time. Show them by example what forgiveness is and how important it is to live an empowered and fulfilled life. Let's face it, if we learn the art of forgiveness we have learnt a key component to a happy, peaceful life. And who better to teach them this first hand than us, their parents.

I always remember my mother teaching me by word and example never to let the sun go down on my anger. I witnessed my parents in conflict when they disagreed, however, I always also witnessed them working through that disagreement to a place of respect, love and common ground before they went to bed at night. They always reached a resolution before their heads hit the pillow and openly told us that they always would, which gave me and my siblings a strong sense of security as a family and as individuals and it was empowering for us all.

I heard someone say once that **one of the best ways to make your children feel loved and secure is to love, respect and value their other parent**. If you are in the position where your child doesn't live with both parents, all is not lost, however make sure you don't speak derogatively about their other parent.

We need to be honest about situations but speaking badly about your child's other parent doesn't make them love you more or them less; it does, however make your child sad and confused.

Rob's father didn't live in the family home in Rob's teenage years and he would be the first one to say that a child soon works out what's right and wrong and which parent can be trusted as they grow up, without any negative talk from someone else.

Let's be parents that create environments where our children can feel safe and secure, learning how to value and respect family members by our example.

Let's create environments that empower our spouses and partners and in turn empower our children, setting them up for a life of love security, purpose and potential.

The Value Of Our Daughters

I thought I would take a moment to talk about the value of our daughters.

Across the globe there are strong messages about the plight of girls – in human trafficking, education and even in simple things such as providing girls in some countries with sanitary napkins so that they can attend school. **Our girls need us.**

This brings me to our daughters, the girls we have been entrusted to raise. Our role as their mothers and fathers is so important. We live in a world in which our girls are bombarded with messages about their sexuality. From a young age it seems that they are told that their value lies in what they bring to the table or leave on the dance floor. Equally so, our boys are being bombarded with images of scantily clad girls, possibly receiving the message that their value doesn't matter. Girls are objects of whatever desire we have.

As I write this, my heart aches for our girls and I'm reminded of how they need us to be strong mothers, grandmothers, aunties who will remind them of exactly who they are and teach them how to walk in the fullness of their internal beauty; because true beauty comes from the gold that lies within all of us.

As a young mother I remember seeing my beautiful little Anna gaze up at me as we walked through the shops or on the beach. I remember seeing her try on my high-heeled shoes and wobble around the lounge room. It was in those moments that I soon learned that my beautiful little girl would get much of her understanding of her value from me. Yes, my hubby, her daddy, Rob, would play a huge part in that, but as her mother she would see me and how I valued myself and in turn how I valued her and taught her to value herself.

Initially, the thought of this was overwhelming. My beautiful Anna, who is now raising children of her own, is surrounded by competing outside influences like Snapchat, Instagram and Tumblr all of which didn't exist when she was growing up. Nevertheless, the fears I had for my Anna were the same as girls have today and the need to instil value upon her was just as great.

Much of my daughter's value came from watching me live and watching me respond to situations – how I carried myself, the words I spoke to others, the words I spoke in private and even the way I spoke about myself. She was gathering and computing all of it. As I watch her today, I see how important those early years were for her. How important it was that I chose to value myself and how I deliberately spoke value over her and into her.

Recently, I was in a conversation with a young mum and I loved how she spoke to her 15-year-old daughter regarding a boy who liked her. Actually, not only did the mother speak to her daughter, she spoke to the boy himself.

Allow me to share her story here; you will see why I cheered her on while she shared it with me:

My young friend found herself in a situation where a 17-year-old boy was interested in her 15-year-old daughter (who, by the way, is drop dead gorgeous!). Her daughter was also interested in him and they had spent time messaging back and forth via Facebook and Snapchat. It became quite obvious that the level of interest was increasing. My friend, being a very engaged mother, monitors her daughter's activity on social media sites (a very wise decision indeed) and she therefore noticed that this young boy had started sending some messages that were totally inappropriate. The messages weren't that bad, but my friend could see where the conversations were headed. This is where the story gets good…

The boy was at their house one day and in front of her daughter, her daughter's friend and the boy, my friend addressed the situation. She told the boy that she had seen what he had sent her daughter and that it was inappropriate. She said that she was disappointed that he would think it appropriate for him to send her daughter anything of that nature. She went on to tell him how valuable her daughter was and how he was going to have to lift his game if he was ever going to have any kind of relationship with her – how **she was worth more than 'risqué Snapchats'** and that she was not a place for him to test the waters of what was appropriate. She went on to tell him that if he wanted to communicate with her, he needed to do it respectfully and that he needed to place value on her. She told him that what he had done placed no value on her, but rather his level of communication told her that she was worth what my friend termed 'gutter talk'.

As my friend had the conversation openly, honestly and in front of him and her daughter's friend, she could see her daughter smiling. She noticed her shoulders were back as she sat up tall and straight, and, in fact, at one point her girlfriend clapped and cheered as my friend questioned him about all the other girls he was chatting to and how that didn't place value on her daughter either. Needless to say, my friend covered all the bases and took this opportunity to drive her point home. After the boy had left (not doubt reconsidering his actions) my friend's daughter wrapped her arms around her mother's neck and thanked her. She thanked her for placing value on her, for not being scared to challenge this boys thinking, for simply letting her know that she cared and that her mother valued her and for letting him know that she was worth so much more than he knew.

I share this story with you to let you know that our girls need us. They need us to:

- Show them what value looks like through our own life – we need to value ourselves
- Walk in the fullness of who we are – fearfully and wonderfully made and chosen for today and entrusted to raise the gorgeous girls that have been entrusted to us
- To place value on them through the words we speak to them and to remind them that they are amazing girls and that true beauty comes from the inside out.

As a mother I have endeavoured to place value on my own daughter and I am very proud of my Anna – she is confident in who she is, and she now places value on her daughters Ruth and Sarah. Anna has also worked with Aboriginal girls, girls in Bali, Indonesia, India and Africa, placing value upon all the unvalued girls in these places.

I want to encourage you to place value on yourself, on the girlfriends in your world and on your beautiful children you have been blessed with to raise. I promise, that when we value others and when we teach and show them how to do that, it helps our daughters to value themselves. Remember that your words matter and your girls need to see and hear you leading the way.

So, the next time your sweet, darling daughter tries to 'walk in your shoes', be reminded that much of her value and her sense of who she is comes from you. What an honour it is for you to place that value on her.

Who knows what our confident daughters will do and places they might go to place that value on vulnerable girls across the globe as they are moved with compassion.

I'm cheering you on and believing in each one of you!

We have included the next chapter in this section on Value because to invade your children's space places value on them – one day they'll agree with you!

Walk A Mile In Their Shoes

As you value yourself and others it's amazing how your world changes.

I find myself thinking about our children and am reminded of all the challenges kids are faced with today. **Unlike any other time in history we are connected in a way that is unprecedented** and it's only going to get more 'invasive'. Yes, connectivity is only going to increase which means the need to connect as family, face-to-face, is possibly more important than ever. As parents you compete with Xbox, iPad, iPhone, FaceTime and the list goes on. With all this connectivity the need to connect in real time and face-to-face if even greater.

The pressure kids are under because of all this connectivity scares me a little. It scares me because they get no rest from their school, extracurricular activities, church, little athletics or whatever group they belong to. The pressure is sometimes hidden from parents, which is why I say we need to 'Walk a Mile in Their Shoes'.

Children are amazing creations. They are simple, yet can be complex. I would suggest that today's society is far more complex than the carefree days we all experienced as children. Think back to your childhood. When you wanted to 'hang' with a friend, you made plans that (in most cases) your parents were aware of. Your connectivity happened for the most part, through the family telephone that for some of us 'more seasoned' people, hung on the kitchen wall and we had to ask permission to use it. Today, things are very different. Children are connected, not only with people in their immediate world who they want to be connected with, but they are also connected with people outside of that space, perhaps with people they don't want to be connected with. In addition to that, they are also connected to people who live far beyond the walls of their home; with people whom they have never, nor will they likely ever, meet face-to-face. These are the people our children meet via social media (if your kids are old enough) or even innocent games and websites like Animal Jam or Minecraft.

Indeed, without us even knowing it, our children can connect with the outside and greater outside world in a way that we never, ever did.

'Walking a Mile in Their Shoes' means engaging with your children and meeting them where they are to **create space and trust for meaningful conversations**. Your children need to know that you understand them. By 'Walking a Mile in Their Shoes' you get the opportunity to see, to hear and to understand more ably the pressures, the joys, the excitement and sadly, the failures your children will and do experience.

Parents, **it's incumbent upon all of us to appropriately invade their space** by engaging with them.

How do you do this? Here are some ideas that have worked for Rob and I through our years of parenting:

1. **Television**

   If they love Peppa Pig, talk about what she does on the show, talk about the other characters and how the story ended up. To keep the conversation going and interesting, tell them what you like about her. This may sound silly, but trust me, it will be part of you setting a strong foundation of mutual interest and respect for each other in the future. If you find this challenging, just think about how adults connect over a conversation about their favourite shows and make it age appropriate.

2. **Cooking**

   Many children love to cook. Set time aside where you can make a mess and cook something together. Let them help with whole process, deciding what to cook, getting out the ingredients and putting it all together. This process involves lots of talking and cooperating. In other words, it is relationship building. Make sure you keep some of what you create for others in the family to enjoy. Also, make sure they are part of the clean-up. This too is part of relationship building. By cooking together you can accomplish something together that you can both be proud of, which is very important. The key word is TOGETHER.

3. **Activities**

   If your children enjoy things like Little Kickers, dancing, gymnastics etc., go the extra mile and get on Google with them and find out lots of interesting things about their interest. Print out some pictures and write out some points about it all, keeping it simple and involving them by gluing the pictures or drawing some. Put them up on the wall or in a book of some kind so they can show other members of the family or friends. You could even write a little story of just a line or two to go with it. This will give them a sense of pride, build their interest and confidence and will build your relationship with them. **The key here is to keep it simple and fun.**

4. **Outings together**

   Take them to special places like sport events such as footy, musicals, local or a trip to the city, perhaps for a visit to the aquarium. Always bring a little something home so they can keep it as a reminder of the outing. Put your little something in a prominent spot and keep referring to the great time you had together. This builds priceless memories for both of you.

5. **Social media (Instagram/Facebook):**
   Put pictures of your good times together and share them on your chosen social media platform. This lets them see how proud you are of the good time you had together and that the time you spent with them mattered. Just watch their little faces shine and their chests swell with pride when you do this.

I can assure you, that as you put the extra effort in while they are young you are building a firm foundation that is easily built upon as they grow. There is a wonderful and true saying that says 'what you sow you will reap'. I believe this and have seen it in my own life. If you want a strong and healthy connection with your children, you need to **be deliberate about it** and go the extra mile. You will never regret it. Rob and I are so glad that we put the extra effort in during those early years because now we are reaping the benefits of having strong, healthy connections with our adult children.

I hope this encourages you to be the parent you hope to be. I've heard it said that we are children for only a short time, yet our childhood stays with us and impacts us for a lifetime.

Enjoy your children.

One of the best ways of showing your children that you enjoy their company is to be tactile about it.

How Touch Impacts A Child's Development

Touch is one of the essential elements of our development. It is a critical component to help our children grow into strong, healthy adults.

Scientists are still discovering the value of touch in a child's physical, emotional and intellectual development. When we touch our children with loving hugs, hold their hands, give them a kiss or just sit next to them while they snuggle, we are helping their development.

Dr Caroline Leaf says that "We each have our natural, inner pharmacy that produces all the drugs we will ever need to run our body-mind in precisely the way it was designed to run. Good touching releases the body's natural chemicals like endorphins, enkephalins, oxytocin and dopamine, setting in motion your love circuits and stopping the fear circuits."

We often take for granted what is happening within our child's little mind and body as we live our everyday lives. We can become too casual and not be deliberate enough in making sure we are giving our children a loving, secure message about our love for them. The way they experience touch with us will not only affect this message about how much we love them, but how much we value them.

When our children are touched in a negative way, of course, we devalue them and create negative thought patterns in their brains, producing ideas that bring ill health as well as adverse effects on their emotional and intellectual development. We all hate hearing of children who have been touched inappropriately and have seen the horrible impact of this.

Lack of contact will also deprive a child of the opportunity to grow to their full potential, even stunting their physical growth. There is a lot of scientific evidence showing how infants in overcrowded orphanages don't grow and develop appropriately for their age. In fact, when I visited an orphanage in Rwanda for the first time in 2012, I witnessed this first hand. It was probably the most confronting day of my life. Rob and I, with three other friends, visited an orphanage that had beautiful, caring, loving carers for the children as there was no lack of love for these children. They were clean, had food to eat, a cot for each to sleep in; there were even smiles on some faces as their carers were lovingly smiling at them.

> *Lack of contact will also deprive a child of the opportunity to grow to their full potential, even stunting their physical growth.*

That all being said, there were nevertheless so many children to care for that the carers had to spend most of their time preparing food, cleaning and keeping the children safe. These demands left little time for a loving touch and one on one time with these precious little ones. While we were there we went from room to room; the staff had grouped the children in their age groups as best they could as most didn't have birth certificates. As we went into the three-to four-year-old rooms the children were just sitting in their cots even though they were able to get out of the cots when not sleeping. We went into what they called the play room. It was tiny and very cramped; there were no toys, just mats on the floor. The children started singing for us; tears were running down all our faces. I was the only female; the others were all fathers and of course Rob a grandfather. We could only fit two of us in the room at a time. Rob and I started to dance with them by just bobbing up and down because of the lack of space and they loved it. These children looked like they were about 18 months to two years old. Their physical development was so stunted because they had been unable to receive regular, loving touches from their carers.

Along with physical development, research shows us that the absence of loving touch causes a change in a child's brain, creating patterns of negative behaviour and of aggression that can lead to violence.

Even as adults we need a loving touch to keep us emotionally and physically well; some like it more than others, but we all need it in our lives.

If you are a parent who isn't very tactile, make sure you don't push your children away when they want a cuddle. You need to learn how to put their needs before your comfort.

My children have had varying degrees of need for touch from me. I had to learn that one of them didn't like too much cuddling, so I had to give it to them only when they wanted it. Another, being very tactile, was often touching me when he was young; he would squeeze my upper arm, feeling the skin in between his fingers. As parents we just need to be patient and learn to read their needs so that we can meet them where they are. **Loving touch needs to be part of their day with us,** even if it's just a hand on their back as we say, 'well done'. I often talk about our words and how they affect our children (we will explore that in a later chapter), but I want us all to remember the importance of touch and how it helps our children and grandchildren reach their full potential.

God created us such complex beings, we all need each other and we need to receive the loving touch from those we love.

The Power Of Saying I'm Sorry And Extending Forgiveness

Did you know that 'I'm sorry' is one of the hardest things to say? And along with 'I'm sorry', 'I need help' is another tough statement.

I would like to talk about the power of forgiveness and how **three little words can change your life** and the lives of the children you are raising.

We all make mistakes. As hard as it is to believe, it's true – you and I make mistakes. We say the wrong thing, we do the wrong thing, we unintentionally hurt people and we even intentionally hurt people. We intentionally cause hurt with our words, which is why I am so passionate about speaking life over people and to people. For now, let's focus on recognising that we all make mistakes. My hope is that as we explore this conversation we will arrive at a place of being okay with saying 'I'm sorry' and extending a hand of forgiveness.

When it comes to saying, 'I'm sorry', we all struggle because it is admitting that we are responsible for what we've done. We are saying 'I was wrong'. It is a vulnerable place; it's exposing and it's hard. Why is it so hard?

I think it's because once we open that door we are giving the person we have hurt permission to either say something back or to perhaps shrug it off, leaving us feeling exposed which then leads to embarrassment. When we say 'I'm sorry' we are hoping to be reconciled with the person; reconciled back to the place we were before the words were spoken.

> *Saying 'I'm sorry' isn't a place of weakness, it is a place of strength.*

Being vulnerable enough about our actions, reactions, words, etc. signifies growth and maturity.

Forgiveness is a big part of talking about saying 'I'm sorry'. Why is forgiveness so important and why is it something we should give? Forgiveness is more about you than it is about the person who hurt you. Giving forgiveness doesn't mean that what the person said or did didn't hurt, it means that you will be okay even though you felt hurt and eventually all will be okay.

Forgiveness is also a place of strength. Being able to extend forgiveness speaks volumes about your character, your mind and your soul. Extending forgiveness is powerful and when given or experienced, it's power knows no end and it truly is more about what happens in you rather than the person you are forgiving.

So, why is it important to teach our kids to say 'I'm sorry' and 'I forgive you'? It's important because life can be tough. Hurtful situations and circumstances will arise; life isn't fair and challenges will present themselves. As parents we know this is true, so showing them by example what saying 'I'm sorry' looks like, what extending forgiveness looks like, is a beautiful life lesson.

I encourage you to be the first to say the words 'I'm sorry' in your homes and to be the one willing to forgive and to let go.

> *Don't be afraid to say 'I'm sorry', to your children.*

It's needed for the times you lose it in the car on the way to school, or after you've stepped on the fortieth piece of Lego that is strewn around the house. Another time is after or during a fight or argument with your partner. This is perhaps one of the best life lessons you will show your children.

> *Walking in forgiveness and using the powerful words of 'I'm sorry' will change your life for the better.*

When our eldest child Ben turned thirteen years old and was struggling to understand this new season in his life and all the changes that were happening for him, he and I started to clash.

We began arguing and butting heads over the simplest things and I couldn't work out why all of a sudden our relationship as a mother and son had turned such a horrible corner. We had always been so close.

As I stopped, reassessed, prayed and sought guidance from someone I respected who was further along on the journey of parenting than me, I started to realise that I couldn't parent a teenager the same way I parented my younger ones.

After realising my mistake, I apologised to Ben and told him how, as this was my first experience parenting a teenager, I still had a lot to learn and I asked him if we could start over.

That apology took all the pressure off our relationship and it got stronger and stronger from that point on.

It's amazing how, when we as parents become vulnerable to our children, we can add so much strength to our relationship with them.

Understanding Our Potential And That Of Our Children

"The only person you are destined to become is the person you decide to be." – Ralph Waldo Emerson.

When I saw this quote, straight away I thought of an amazing young man who has no legs or arms. He has a torso and one flap on one side of his torso that resembles a foot. His name is Nick Vujicic and he has written a book called *Life Without Limits*. He is one person who you could easily believe doesn't have much to look forward to in life. It would seem to most people that it would be impossible for him to have much of a destiny at all and yet this young man has achieved much more than most able-bodied people, including myself.

This man just blows my mind; it almost seems unreal as you watch him. He obviously has help from people, but his belief in his potential and future is just outstanding. He lives a life full of hope and joy, his achievements are enormous and it just leaves me dumbfounded when I learn about all he has achieved.

The list of all that he is able to do is long and includes surfing, snowboarding and so much more. I strongly encourage you to investigate his story and share it with your family. He is one of the most inspiring people I have encountered. I've been told that when he speaks to students he talks about having a bad day and that if anyone was allowed to have a bad day it would be him. But he chooses not to, and he speaks openly about how he makes his way through those moments in his life.

Nick was born in Australia, but lives in America now and I first heard of him when I saw him on TV a few years ago. When I saw and heard him, I was captivated and I found it hard to believe at first, but the evidence is right there in front of you. He's there, speaking and sharing his truth. Following my first glimpse of him, I bought his book and couldn't put it down as it was so compelling to read. I would love you to buy it and read it and to allow Nick's story to awaken your potential. Let the story stir you up so that you can **deposit that belief of limitless potential into your children.**

It is so easy to look at our circumstances, whether good or bad, and let them limit us and our children. Did you know that sometimes when parents have done well themselves, their success can intimidate their children and squash their potential? On the flip side, did you know that when parents haven't reached their desired level of success, they limit their children's potential by not expecting their children to go beyond where they have gone themselves? And, did you know that some parents don't want their children to exceed them because of pride? Again, on the flip side, did you know that parents can push their children to succeed so much that it can be soul destroying? This usually comes out of fear and wanting their children to achieve and not struggle in life. Understanding and helping our children walk in their full potential is a very delicate balance. A starting point always has to be our honest motivation and our ability to believe for the best result, knowing deep within us that they are full of potential.

I can remember my own mum and dad always speaking of my potential and believing that without a doubt I would do well in life. Let me share a short story with you: when I was in high school, my headmistress decided to tell my mother where she expected me to end up. This 'telling' didn't sit very well with my lovely mother. It wasn't an encouraging end to my life story. My mum told her exactly what she thought of her comments to me – that she apparently didn't know me or my potential. As far as Mum was concerned I would become a woman of worth and would achieve well. In saying this, Mum always supported the teachers when they disciplined me, as I often needed it. Plus, my mother always gave me the appropriate punishment when I was in trouble at school; she never let me off the hook. There were always consequences for my actions. However, **my mother always believed in me and that I would amount to something and so I believed it too.** I have a good friend, Susan, who tells of her mother and I quote her: "She spoke potential into me and helped me to see it for myself."

What we expect of our children's future is what they will usually become as adults. So, be careful with your expectations. Lift them high, for yourself, your spouse and your children and you will be surprised with the result. When you believe in your children, it won't matter what other people say to them or about them, because their future is secure. Professionals and friends can say what they like, your child will believe you before they believe them.

> *You have the biggest impact on your children's destiny.*

Nick was born with what looked like huge limitations. I can only imagine how all the staff in the hospital would've thought that he wouldn't achieve much. I wonder if his parents were devastated. I can't even begin to understand what it was like for them. I do know that they must be amazing people with great strength and determination. Parents who vowed to never give up on their son. I want to try and imagine what their situation must have been like. What others must have been saying and speaking over their precious baby boy. Their strength inspires me. They would have questioned what his life would or could look like. There would have been so many questions dancing around in their minds. They were determined to give him a normal life – a new normal. That wee baby who was born with some of the greatest challenges was blessed with parents who could see beyond the physical. They could see the potential of what could be and who he could be.

As I listen to Nick speak and read his words, it's apparent to me that **his belief in his potential was an excellent foundation** and he has lived what is truly an extraordinary life. Again, I encourage you to Google him and learn about his incredible story.

Every parent who has children, able-bodied or not, with or without learning difficulties, should read his book and read through it with your children. Teach them to take the limits off what life and people love to put on us. I must tell you that faith plays a part in his journey. It has in mine and my family's as well. I believe that the Creator has filled every one of us with potential beyond our dreams. Believe in your potential and believe in your children's potential no matter what the circumstances.

Decide who you want to be and go for it! Give your children permission to dream big and decide what they wish to achieve in life. Then believe it with them and enjoy the ride.

LOVE is Spelled TIME

We've been talking about identity and self-esteem and building it into our children. I've been thinking about how much we all love our children and how we express love to them.

Of course we tell them, but do we tell them often enough? We show them with hugs and cuddles, but do we show them enough? Love is an interesting emotion that can be felt, seen and heard. Love is experienced on so many levels, whether it is a knowing glance or gaze, a soft touch or a kind word. To have loved and to have known love is a precious thing and something we should never take for granted.

So why is love sometimes spelled TIME? When it comes to our children, this is often the most tangible way for them to understand love. It has been said that time is a great healer and time is a great revealer.

> *Time spent with your children will heal, will reveal and will draw them to you.*

Your time is possibly one of your greatest expressions of love that they will carry with them throughout their lives. You see, people never forget how you make them *feel* and by spending time with your children they will *feel* love.

When summer comes, use the extra hours of sunshine to spend time with those you love and cherish. Take the kids to the beach before or after work; start getting up that little bit earlier and go for a walk, a swim or jump on your bikes. Go fishing and relax into the evening sunsets with your kids. You will never regret the time spent with them, but trust me, you will regret the time you didn't.

Children love being outside and they love having fun with their parents. They actually love seeing us laughing and being silly sometimes. I understand that our schedules can be busy and that the demands on life are at times very big, but when the weather is good, please grab hold of the opportunity to explore your outdoor spaces with your family. Allow the extra time weekends afford us to enhance your family relationships

In this age of technology and connectivity, I realise how easy it is to let children spend their time engaged in online activities through games, the Xbox, Wii or PlayStation and others. As compelling and captivating as these activities are to children, I can guarantee you they will jump at the opportunity to spend some quality time with you doing simple things like:

- Going to the beach and building a sandcastle
- Going on a bushwalk or a picnic
- Bike rides
- Building something in the garage
- Finding a basketball court and play a game
- Planting a veggie or herb garden
- Baking or cooking something new and exciting for a family dinner.

These are simple, inexpensive ways to enjoy time together as a family.

Our children were raised on the Central Coast of New South Wales and I remember how Rob and I enjoyed spending hours on the beach with our children. The laughter coupled with the roar of the ocean, the sun-kissed smiles, the hot chips or sandy picnic lunches and a tired drive home equalled a day well spent. Some of our best memories are from days like this when the weather started to feel more like summer and we shed our layers for our beach towels and threw caution to the wind and enjoyed one another.

Turn the phone and computer off, silence the outside noise and simply enjoy your family and **build memories that will last a lifetime**.

Love is spelled time. This is a little something I like to remind myself of and I hope you will enjoy it too:

> There is a time and season for everything; a time to be born and a time to die, a time to plant and a time to uproot, a time to kill and a time to heal, a time to tear down and a time to build, a time to weep and a time to laugh, a time to mourn and a time to dance, a time to scatter stones and time to gather them, a time to embrace and time to refrain from embracing, a time to search and a time to give up, a time to keep and time to throw away, a time to tear and time to mend, a time to be silent and a time to speak, a time to love and time to hate, a time for war and a time for peace.

My prayer for your families is that you make the time to enjoy the moments together; that in and through the time spent together you will breathe life into one another and see your identities and self-esteems being built up.

Each Child Is Unique

As parents it's so important to see each one of our children as unique and special in their own right.

I wasn't always good at drawing these unique qualities out in my children. I remember the comments I would make about how one or the other was like Rob or myself or even like one of my siblings. There is nothing wrong with that, however, I believe I did it too much in the early days. I believe it can unintentionally devalue each child's uniqueness.

Whilst there will always be characteristics our children will inherit through our complex DNA, over time I have learned that it is important to focus more on the person that they are, unique and wonderful, rather than on who they share a likeness with.

A few years ago, at Little Miracles, a child made a statement that has stayed with me over the years. He said, **"I am the boss of my own name."** I instantly loved the strong statement and the fact that he simply knew who he was and there was no question or space to question him. He was the boss of his name.

I pondered this at the time, and still do. It reminds me of something I have read in Scripture where it is written that we are all 'God's masterpiece'.

> *What a beautiful thought – we are a true masterpiece.*

This would suggest that we are all originals, and although we may share traits and characteristics with others, we are originals. I think about the art world and how originals are always of more value and are highly sought after. This is true about us and our children. The original is where the beauty and truth lie and it's important to remember that it is the original that attracts the attention, not the copy or a similar one.

As I said above, in the early days I often told my children how much they resembled others in our family. Additionally, my four children have always been told (by others) how much they all look alike. Over the years there have been many occasions when people have glanced over and mistaken Ben and Michael for one another. Yes, they resemble each other greatly, yet I realise how truly unique they all are. None of them are the same and all have amazing features and qualities that are so special and make up who they are as individuals. In all of our individual uniqueness, we compliment the unity that we know as family. I'm sure many of you have come to understand this as well. Although your child/ren resemble either you or your partner, your parents or siblings, or one another, we are quick to learn that there is so much more to a person than the similarities. In fact, as I said before, it is their originality that makes them wonderfully and uniquely 'them'. As a grandparent I see resemblances run through the family line. It's actually amazing to watch.

Like the little boy who blessed us at Little Miracles with the confidence of being the boss of his name, it is so important that we all speak to our children about their unique qualities and help them recognise the beauty of those qualities for themselves. We need to celebrate them. As I said earlier, I haven't always been good at this, but all is not lost. I learned along the way to be better at it and have become quite deliberate about it. Over the years of parenting, I have learned that we will never get it right all the time; however, we can always learn and put our new lessons into place.

In this regard I'd like to share a few observations from my own family with you.

Ben has always been a natural at long distance running, surfing, reading people and truly engaging with people. He also had a huge imagination and as an adult this imagination has helped him invent and create. As a child it definitely kept me on my toes!

Anna was always good at making sure everyone was looked after and that no one was treated unfairly. As a teenager she was always amazing with children and able to relate to them in a special way. This of course is a huge asset in childcare. Anna is also very creative and loves to create with children.

Michael was always very good at soccer, surfing and most sports. He always had a natural ability to work out how things were put together and how they worked. He never read instructions; I just gave him whatever needed to be put together and he worked it out. This always came in very handy as Rob has never been a handyman around the house. Thank God for Michael!

Daniel has always had a great discernment when it comes to people. He can smell a fake from a mile away. He is a great listener, has less to say, but when he speaks wisdom spills out from him and he is captivating. He too loves sport and is good across the board.

These are, of course, just a few examples of their fabulous strengths and abilities; there are many more.

I share all this with you because I've learned that as parents Rob and I have become very deliberate in seeking to understand and recognise each child's uniqueness and to celebrate it with them. This takes time, listening, observing and lots of patience. Then, once you've figured them out, it takes time helping them develop their unique strengths by taking them to the sports, acting classes, sometimes to Sydney (an hour or two away) or beyond for activities. Learning how to cheer them on without pushing them too far is all part of the challenge too. When they learn as children how valuable they are and how unique they are, they will be more confident and will be in a position to be able to value one another's uniqueness.

> *Your child is the original – celebrate that!*

Don't try and make them what they aren't or what you feel comfortable with them being. Don't live your dreams through them. Look, listen and learn what makes them unique and draw that out of them. Champion them on to be their own masterpiece, a one of a kind that no one can copy. Model this for them by doing all you can to be happy with who you are. This may mean some better thought patterns, perhaps even talking to a professional and getting some counselling so that you can sort out some of your baggage, if you have any. Be free to be you and celebrate the uniqueness of the individuals in your home. Let the uniqueness in everyone be the ingredient that shapes the culture of your family.

Ben, Anna, Michael and Daniel have always been told they can achieve anything that they desire; each one of their spouses are told the same thing by Rob and myself and now we are cheering on our 12 grandchildren.

Some tips for the journey

1. Find out what they love, encourage them before they become really good at it; stretch them, empower them, expose them to ways of developing the gifts they were born with.

2. Take them out of their comfort zones while still being their safety net.

3. Show them how much you value their uniqueness and how it helps to complement your family.

4. Talk to your extended family and ask them to celebrate and encourage your children. The more affirmation they get, the more confidence they will experience. If you don't have extended family that can do this, I am sure you have friends who can.

5. Tell their preschool teacher and school teacher the unique gifts you see your child having and watch them start to recognise it. They may even be able to point out more to you that they observe.

6. Believe in your child's uniqueness, speak it into them and over them; be genuine, not pushy, but always celebrate it.

7. Remember that we are all God's masterpiece, a one of a kind, of huge value that can never be repeated.

8. **Be you and set the world on fire; allow your child to be themselves, celebrating their uniqueness and watch them make you proud to be their parents as they set their world on fire!** We are all given our uniqueness to add value to our world, family and friends and beyond. Help them see how their uniqueness is needed and how it makes a difference to them and everyone else when they live it out.

The Danger Of Comparison

Parenting is a difficult but very rewarding job. There are days or nights when we lay our head on our pillow, confident that we have done a great job. Then there are days when we shed a tear as we close the door on another day. Those are the days when we are unsure, confused and simply trying our best to keep our head above water. Either day is okay; things happen and thankfully, 'Tomorrow is another day'.

As I think about parenting, I have come to know and understand that one of the big things that can cause insecurity and uncertainty is the age-old problem of comparison. **Comparison can be lethal** and it can cause wreckage, wherever it travels.

I'd like to share a story with you, one that comes directly from the pages of my own family story. I hope you enjoy this honesty. I share it in an effort to see you move forward with confidence.

Every year Rob and I take the entire family away, all 22 of us, so that we can relax, away from the demands of life and simply enjoy one another's company. The grandchildren enjoy the freedom the break brings and the adults look forward to late night card games, many chats and much laughter. Yes, it can be hectic with so many of us, but I wouldn't change it for the world. This is a week I look forward to all year.

As you can well imagine, a holiday with 22 people, all with different personalities and an age range of 11 weeks to 69 years, definitely presents its challenges. It becomes very evident, even within the same extended family that there are differences in many areas, but especially (I found) in parenting styles. I must add though that differences are good and healthy. Imagine if we were all the same... not very exciting.

On one of our days away, we travelled to Kiama to play around the amazing Blowhole. What fun! Needless to say we all got wet as water spurted out of the hole. I wish you could have heard the squeals of joy and laughter that came from the grandchildren. I'm not sure what I enjoyed more – the magic of the Blowhole or the sound of my grandchildren loving the moment.

The day continued with a picnic on the grass with hot chips and fresh bread (who said holidays need to be full of green veggies?!). After our lazy lunch the others went to the next activity and I took the opportunity to rest and enjoy some time with my beautiful grandson, Noah, then only 11 weeks old. Whilst playing with this beautiful child, my lovely daughter-in-love, Leanne, joined me and we had an extraordinary conversation.

Leanne began to share with me a few thoughts in regard to the mother she was. As she spoke, I was reminded of my early days of parenting. The questions, the concerns, the dreams and the desire to do it all right. Leanne spoke about our daughter (her sister-in-love), Anna. She told me how she sees Anna doing such amazing things with her children. Things like taking them on bushwalks and discovering all sorts of treasures; finding lady beetles and pinecones from trees; discovering rocks to break up and use to paint and create pictures. Her list went on and admiration of Anna and all she was doing with her children was obvious. I could hear and see that Leanne had begun to doubt herself and the mother she was. Leanne was comparing her mothering abilities and skills with that of Anna's. It was interesting to see that, as we talked, Leanne began to understand that she gets excited about other things and although the bushwalks may not be in her children's futures (maybe Aunty Anna will take them on one), her children find extreme pleasure in the things that she does do with them. It's just different, and that's okay!

Leanne is an amazing mother of three and she has a beautiful way of speaking life into her children. She is a caring mother who plays with her children in other ways. Her children are a true credit to her. They are happy, very confident little children who totally enjoy life. They also have lovely manners. Like all children they lose the plot at times, but they bring such joy to our family. Leanne is doing a great job.

As we continue on this journey of parenting I hope you're able to see the picture I'm attempting to paint. There are differences, but to be different is really good. The danger comes when we start comparing ourselves with someone else and wishing we were the same, instead of appreciating and valuing our differences.

> *Differences are healthy!*

Let me tell you about our gorgeous Jenelle who is our first daughter-in-love. Jenelle's mothering is different again. She and our son Ben have two adorable teenage girls plus they have a vibrant little seven-year-old who dazzles us. Jenelle is an empowering mother and her older girls are an absolute pleasure to have around and the younger one is just dynamite.

As Leanne and I sat chatting on the grass that day, she recognised that she will do things differently to Anna and Jenelle and that's okay. Leanne's recognition of this, I believe, is crucial to not only being successful at parenting, but also to enabling her to enjoy being a parent. Don't compare yourself to anyone else and how they go about living their life. This is a trap that robs us of the joy of parenting. Beware, as it is an easy trap to find yourself in because our desire to do this job well is so strong. The trap is easy to fall into because there is so much at stake. We become so critical of ourselves and begin to fear failure. Try and remember 'you only fail when you fail to try'. Don't let your fear of failure take you off the course you are on.

Back to Leanne for a moment... Leanne is the best mum for her children when she is just herself and when she is not trying to compete with or measure up to others; when her focus is on her children rather than the need to 'get it right all the time'. Her motherly instincts are fantastic, which is why her children are so happy. A bushwalk isn't going to change this. She knows herself and her children and walking in that confidence makes her perfect for the job at hand.

As a grandmother I love watching the way my children and their spouses raise our grandchildren. Rob and I have complete confidence in their parenting skills. They all do it differently and different to the way Rob and I did it. In saying that however, there is a common thread which is UNCONDITIONAL LOVE. With this in common, differences are celebrated.

It's great to learn from each other, share tips and give each other support as long as you are free to be YOU and your children are free to be themselves. Don't compare your parenting skills. You will either come up short or you will be very sure others are doing it all wrong and become judgemental. Neither is healthy and will bring a negative result for you and your children.

As I said, my grandchildren are all loved unconditionally and life is spoken over them and the gold within them is being brought to the surface by their parents. This is the foundation of healthy parenting. How each set of parents digs for the gold can be different and that's OK.

Mums, we are the most susceptible to comparing ourselves to others – we have all done it at times, especially when we are at the beginning of our journey. Be confident that you and your child were put together deliberately and on purpose, for a purpose. When you are the best version of yourself, YOU are the best mum for your child. We can always grow in our parenting skills and for me in my grand parenting skills, however, **being YOU is what is best for your child**.

Community

> The strength of a nation derives from the integrity of the home.
>
> **Confucius**

Community = Family

I have had the awesome privilege of visiting Rwanda. Whilst there I was touched by their sense of community and how they gather together with such strength. There is a real sense of family and connectedness within this country which is, literally, building from the ground up.

Seeing this I was reminded of our communities; the ones we live in – the soccer, netball, dance and art communities. In all these communities that you are involved in, you share something in common with others that binds you together. Whether that is sport, perhaps even a wine club, a dinner or a book club – **whatever you share in common binds you together and creates a community.**

So, I would like to pose a question to you: in your immediate community, which is your family, what is the common thread that binds you together? (Yes, your first community is your family although sadly, many don't see family as a community, but I assure you it is.)

Community looks different for many families. It could be surfing or maybe hiking or bushwalking. To others it may be early Saturday morning cycling trips, or it could be cooking or baking or coming together around food, music or even certain kinds of movies.

One of the most important activities as a family is having meals together. There are so many strong cultures right around the world that are built around participating in meals together. We have always been very careful to create meal times where, as a family we can relax and enjoy each other's company.

When our children were young we always ate as a family at the family dinning table through the week. Weekends we often had much more casual eating around the television or around everyone's busy weekend schedule that included sport etc. Now all our children are grown and have their own families we still value the importance of connecting around a meal and so Monday nights are Family Night Dinner nights.

There is no pressure for any family who may not be able to attend at times, however most weeks we are all there together. The children get very disappointed if for some reason we are not able to meet together and they have to wait until the next week. It can be quite hectic with lots of noise, lots of excitement as all the grandchildren love being together and create all sorts of games and adventures together. There can be quite a mess created too, but it can always be cleaned up; that's easily fixed.

It's just wonderful to hear the children's stories of the week and to see them engaging with their aunts and uncles telling them what's been happening in their world. I love watching the teenage girls sitting with the adults having meaningful conversations and also having lots of laughs as they join in on our conversations.

We all get to hear what is happening in the very interesting and challenging lives of teenage girls and how their studies are going. The adults are able to share things of trivia and things of importance, things that they are concerned about and things they find just straight out funny. At times there needs to be some refereeing which is part of the whole journey as the children learn social skills with their cousins.

To create a safe environment like this where such important life skills like respect, turn-taking, listening to others and engagement are learnt so naturally, is priceless.

The point is, meeting regularly together around a meal as a family unit brings us all together and creates a sense of strong culture and community that also creates confidence and a strong sense of belonging for us all.

It might take up a few hours each Monday for me to prepare the meal for all of us, however it's worth every minute and bit of effort as we create that strong bond between us all.

Sport has been a big part of community for Rob and our three sons as together they enthusiastically support their teams. For Anna and I we share a love for people. They fascinate us and we love blessing the people in our world.

Whatever your common thread looks like, can I encourage you to let it weave deeply throughout your family.

> *Build your family community around common interests.*

Find something that draws you all together, something that helps you establish a community that is on the same team. If you don't have one, create one as it's never too late. Trust me when I say this is something you will never regret.

As I think about Rwanda and about how rich their family life is, I remember also the history of that nation and that their strong communities are built on great forgiveness. When I come home from a visit, I come home inspired to keep my community strong.

Community = Family.

The Family Code Of Conduct

I believe it is wise to have a FAMILY CODE OF CONDUCT.

In this age of technology and because of the amount of connectivity your children have, I can see it helping you as you discipline your children and as you help them grow and develop into the wonderful people you have been blessed to raise. Providing healthy, meaningful structure will help you as you endeavour to build your family. **It erases confusion and provides stability in the home**. As you read this, I want to remind you that the code needs to add value to your family and it needs to let everyone know that they are significant. If done correctly, it should be an empowering tool for the family as a whole, as well as each individual family member.

I have heard it said that **if you stand for nothing you are at risk of falling for anything**. What a powerful thought and an extremely bold statement.

As I think about this statement, I find myself thinking about my own life and our family and how important it is that Rob and I established values and beliefs within us as well as in our home. Not only do we need to establish them, but we need to live them ourselves and implement them in our children's lives. Having done so I can see how our family has been saved from situations and circumstances simply because we knew exactly what we stood for personally and corporately as a family.

As a young mother I was determined that my husband and I would raise strong, confident and compassionate children. We realised that in order to do so, we had to make some rules and create boundary lines for our children, providing them with space to grow and mature. We needed to create a culture in our home so that our children knew what we stood for. We needed to create a foundation on which our children could confidently stand.

This brings me to the CODE OF CONDUCT.

What is it?

According the dictionary it is '*a set of conventional principles and expectations that are considered binding on any person who is a member of a particular group.*' Considering this statement helped us understand what a code of conduct was, and we decided that we needed to establish a FAMILY CODE OF CONDUCT of our own.

This allowed each family member the ability to know exactly what we as a family stood for and what the expectations were for everyone in the family. Consequently, the grey areas are erased, everyone is on solid, common ground and together our family moved forward, learning and growing together.

It is important to note that we weren't naïve enough to think that something like this would save us from possible heartache, pain and tears that were shed over the years. However, I do believe that when there is a common goal and thread that brings us together as families, **when we know what we stand for, falling for anything else is a lot harder**. When we come face to face with the possibility of falling, it's in that moment that we hear that still small voice that calls us back and helps us stand in the midst of craziness, strangeness, darkness and confusion.

Whatever the age of your children, talk to them and together establish your own FAMILY CODE OF CONDUCT.

When creating a code of conduct have everyone, even little ones, share what kind of environment or atmosphere they would like to live in within the home.

Depending on the ages of the participants the engagement with the process will vary, but with guidance, you will be surprised at how effective this is.

Ask questions like:

1. What makes you feel loved and valued (what makes you feel safe/ happy)?
2. How do you think we can all show each other respect and add value to each other?
3. What makes you feel devalued and unloved (what makes you feel sad/ unhappy)?
4. What do you need from your family members to be able to enjoy being a valued member of this your family?
5. How can we help you reach your full potential?
6. What do you feel is your responsibility to other members of this family?
7. How can we all be kept accountable to keep the family code of conduct?
8. What are the consequences when the code of conduct is broken?
9. How do we restore the code of conduct once it has been broken?

You may think of other questions that suit your family and of course we always ask questions age appropriately. Whatever you do don't dismiss any answers, sometimes you may need to dig a little deeper always treating the answers with respect, even if they throw you a curve ball.

Write out a copy and have each person be aware of it and change or add to it as children grow and circumstances change.

We as a Bateman family developed a very bad habit of not waiting 'till others had finished what they were saying before we added our bit. It was unintentionally devaluing each other because when this happened we weren't always feeling heard. When it became apparent to us all, we had to learn how to stop and listen much more carefully to each other. This wasn't easy and we are still all working on perfecting it, however, just being aware and having a code around it, we are all showing much more value and honour towards each other and we will keep improving I am sure.

Involving Our Children In Our Successes

We have all heard of families where the parents are very successful, and the children find it hard to live in the shadow of that success. I believe we can dispel the shadow and empower our children to be a part of our success and empower them to live a satisfying, successful life themselves.

I have read many stories of children not coping well with their parents' success; however I know of others who thrive because of successful parents. I would like to encourage you with the treasures I have recognised and learnt on our own journey and that of our friends.

We all need to shoot for the stars, putting our best foot forward and attempting to reach our full potential and succeed in life.

As parents and grandparents, we need to put some measuring points in our lives to help our children journey the road of success with us well. While you are young and working hard to succeed, your family is young and developing their self-awareness, so you need to be conscious of involving them in your dreams. At the same time you can help them imagine and dream for themselves. If you only focus on your goals, what your dreams look like and how to get there, you may unintentionally devalue your children or your spouse.

I believe that when we involve our children in the process and ask for their input along the way, they will become excited and feel part of the success instead of feeling they are living in the shadow of our successes.

Even for small children we can break the intricacies of the process down to their size and ask for their input. Talk to them about what you are doing, asking them what they think about it. Ask them how they feel about the long days you might have to put in to achieve your dreams.

Listen to their words and reflect on them as you help them see they are more important to you than your success, however you have dreams like they do and sometimes it will take a bigger commitment for a period of time to make them come true. Help them see that you see them as part of that success and how you will share the rewards with them.

Be deliberate about taking the children to your workplace; show them around and explain what you are dreaming about and achieving. Explain how things work. Help them understand what it's like for you as you pursue your dreams, what risks you are taking and what you are giving up to achieve them. When you include them they will feel valued and not excluded from the process.

As you talk about your dreams, always encourage your children that they are full of potential and that their dreams are very important to you and you will always believe in their dreams and do all you can to help them achieve them.

I have found that the children who haven't been able to cope with their parent's success are usually feeling undervalued because of lack of one on one time with their parents. They haven't been able to be part of the journey with the parent and so have had no sense of inclusion which then makes them feel devalued.

Make sure you also set time aside to just have fun with them doing whatever makes them happy, which may not necessarily be an activity that you want to do. Do something that they choose on a regular basis. It doesn't have to be every week but often enough for them to know that they are important to you and you enjoy being with them.

> *Take them out of the shadow and put them in the*
> *spotlight of your affection and your dreams.*

Go for your dreams big time! However, include your children in those dreams and help them with their own and celebrate both together.

The Importance Of Grandparents

As a mother of four children I understand the importance of grandparents and how they play an integral role in the raising of our children.

I remember the times when I called upon my mother for either wisdom or for an extra pair of hands to make the days and challenges easier. Now, as a grandparent myself I have an even richer understanding of the role grandparents play – how we can help in not only practical ways, but how we influence our children and grandchildren.

I think back to the days when money was tight and time seemed so short. There were days when it felt like I constantly went from one thing to another; from feeding to changing multiple nappies to attending to cuts and bruises. Sometimes it felt like the days bled into one another and simply rolled by without me knowing what the actual day or the week or date was on the calendar. There were days when Rob and I would call on our parents for (as I mentioned above) practical help and then there were days when I just needed a piece of wisdom. Perhaps it was solving a sibling dispute or figuring out how to keep my sanity whilst children seemingly ruled the roost.

Whatever the case, I am grateful for our parents and the support and wisdom they shared with us. As a grandparent I am endeavouring to do the same for our children.

I encourage you to explore this relationship in a greater way. As I write this, I'm reminded of the African proverb that says 'It takes a village to raise a child'. **Grandparents are a valuable asset** and trust me when I say, we love to be included and involved in our grandchildren's lives. I pray that your relationships go from strength to strength.

Grandparents can add another level of unconditional love to your children; **do all you can to encourage a strong bond between them.** The extended family is such an important component of your child's confidence. If you don't have grandparents nearby, see if there are older neighbours or friends you can involve in the lives of your children.

Games Night

I enjoy the chill in the air on winter evenings.

As I think about this season and how different the seasons are when it comes to family life, I find myself travelling down memory lane. I recall winter nights when our kids were young and how we needed to keep the fun happening. With active boys in the house and my beautiful little girl I can assure you we had a busy home, whatever the season. When winter brings earlier sunsets and prohibitive cold, it meant many nights tucked up inside building forts out of blankets and pillows, hot chocolates and warm bubble baths.

In addition to all of these fun things, we also played games and this is something I want to write about in this chapter. Games nights are some of my favourite memories and I hope you will adopt and build this into your life as well. Winter offers the perfect opportunity to pull out games like Candyland, Monopoly, Articulate Junior or even bonfire Charades. Whatever your children's ages, there are great games that can be played and truly enjoyed, not just endured, by parents.

One of my younger girlfriends longs for this time of year simply because she loves cooking winter food for her family which she lovingly calls 'soul food'. Plus, they have games night throughout the week and extended games on the weekend. She truly believes that this is something that is pulling her family together and I would have to agree with her.

So, can I encourage you to do some or any part of the following:

Get your kids up in their favourite winter jammies, pop some popcorn, make some hot chocolate or even cook some damper on an outdoor firepit and enjoy a night together playing games. I promise you, you will enjoy it and your kids will be crying for more.

There is **something unique that happens when parents engage with their children** (whatever their age) through games. Children are able to see their parents having fun, perhaps even being a little silly at times. Games bring out the child and the competitive person in all of us. So, whether it be a board game or even a Wii game, through this playtime we are allowing our children an opportunity to see us (their parents) relax and have fun. A different kind of fun that perhaps they haven't seen before.

Now, the great thing about a night like this is that it doesn't break the bank and you don't have to go overboard. Keep it simple. You can consider inviting another family over to join in the fun. Sometimes the simplest of things is what brings our families together.

Here is a small list of some great games we and friends have enjoyed (always read age-appropriate labels):

Candyland
Snakes and Ladders
Monopoly
Guesstures
Taboo
Playing Cards (Cheat, Spoons)
Articulate Junior or Regular
Headbands
Scrabble
Boggle

Have fun and enjoy one another.

Developing Lasting Relationships With Our Children

In this chapter I'd love to start the conversation about our relationships with our children and how important it is to keep lines of communication open so that our children know there is always a soft place to land when life gets hard. Recently in Australia we had the 'R U OK?' day and I think that's a great way to remind us to:

1. STOP
2. LOOK AROUND AT THOSE IN OUR WORLD
3. ASK IF EVERYONE IS OKAY

Perhaps you find it odd to suggest asking your children how they are doing. Some wonder how, at the tender age of our little ones, their life could be anything but pleasant. Well, can I tell you that according to 'Youth Beyond Blue', 160 000 young people (16–24 years) in Australia live with depression and around one in six young people have anxiety. Those are staggering numbers and I don't share them to scare you, rather to encourage and empower you and to hopefully put some tools in your 'parenting toolbox' when it comes to connecting with your children.

Thought life
Considering these statistics, although they are referring to 16–24 years of age, I want to encourage you to **engage in conversation with your little ones about their thought life**. Ask questions like:

"What have you been thinking about lately?"
"Are you happy?"
"What makes you feel happy and excited?"
"Is there anything that's bothering you right now?"
"How's your heart feeling?"

These are all questions kids can relate to. They know the feeling of excitement, happiness (the lead up to Christmas or birthdays, etc.). Additionally, they know that things can bother them, especially if they have siblings. Asking how their heart is causes them to use descriptive words to tell you what's going on. Be prepared for them to also ask you questions about what you're asking them. This is a real conversation.

All of these conversations lead into the deeper spaces of their little minds and hearts, allowing you the opportunity to really get an understanding of where they are.

These are big questions and the intent is to help you, as their parent, to gain a better understanding of what they are feeling. It's also a good habit to get into. In this, they are being taught to ask themselves that question which will serve them well in their teens and beyond. Perhaps some of us adults could benefit from asking these internal questions. I know I can!

Creating Time and Space for Conversation

Parenting requires time and patience (trust me, with four children this is something I came to understand and know well). Finding time to listen to your children can be challenging as our days are full of work, activities, home duties and everything else. In saying that, can I encourage you to find time to give them your full attention, **creating space for** what you will soon discover are **incredible conversations.** Here are just a few suggestions from my 'Parenting Toolbox'…

The drive home in the car:
I always found this to be a great time of sharing, chatting and catching up on all the day's activities. Start this whilst they are little and perched up in their car seat/booster seat, and you will reap the benefits now and during the teen years. Important to note: I also found driving their friends around a real bonus as well, because the stories I overheard were amazing. I learnt many important things about my children and their friends by saying nothing and just listening to their conversations. These provided me with valuable nuggets for when we were alone and chatting. This drive time with your children can be some of the most rewarding times you will spend with them. And you may as well enjoy it as there are many hours on the road ahead.

Bedtime/story Time:
We are passionate about teaching our children to read and the bedtime reading routine is often a great opportunity to relax and chat with your little one. After the 'book of choice' has been read, simply relax into that space and begin to marvel at the day that's just gone and the day that lies ahead. Let the unwinding take place and in most cases you will be surprised at how much they want and are willing to share. Again, creating this space will bode well for these years and the teen years ahead.

Our relationship with our children is so important. I want to encourage you to spend time with them, listening and absorbing what they bring to the conversation. Children want to know they are being heard, that they are safe and that they are secure. As parents we have the incredible opportunity to show them and to let them feel all of those things.

These are obviously just a few little tips and strategies I have used over the years all in an effort to raise healthy, happy children. Ultimately, building relationships with the children I have been blessed and trusted to raise. As a mother of older children now I don't regret a moment spent listening to them and their stories.

Hopefully these tips from my 'Parenting Toolbox' will help you to create the relationship you want with your child and the relationship your child wants with you… I'm cheering you on all the way!

Moving Out Of Your Comfort Zone

As a team-building exercise, our company's Little Miracles Early Learning Center teams on the Central Coast of New South Wales ventured out to the TreeTops Adventure Park. The park is situated at Yarramalong on the Central Coast, not far off the freeway. It's a place of excitement, tranquillity, fun, big challenges and definitely a space where you are taken out of your comfort zone.

In terms of team-building, it certainly hit the mark; it was a wonderful exercise. Those who seemed the more fearless or had higher fitness levels cheered the others on. Some of us found the challenges quite confronting and although the cheer squad was there, we too needed a verbal push along as we conquered our physical giants.

As a more 'seasoned' woman I find myself lost in the excitement and the challenge of days like this. Although I find myself asking 'what am I doing, get me out of here, I will never do this again!', I inevitably find myself, year after year, climbing one more wall, running a course or whatever the case may be. I think I love these days and challenges because I recognise the importance of being 'out of my comfort zone'. I embrace this because after a few years on this planet and being determined to make a difference for the generations to come, I realise that **in order to live the life I dream of, I need to grow as a person.** These days are perfect boundary pushers.

Throughout the day and as we embraced new and ever-increasing challenges, I found myself lost in the spirit of the Little Miracles team.

I realised that the spirit and culture of honour that we are committed to and instil in our children, has become a reality within our staff team. Yes, we cheered each other on and encouraged each other on to new heights, but it wasn't only our team we focused on – we encouraged the team ahead and cheered relentlessly as they accomplished new heights. My heart was warmed as I watched our team building each other up and others who came along our path simply because of the culture of honour we have committed ourselves to live by. What a privilege it was to get a glimpse of how something as simple as speaking about and exampling honour can impact lives.

Along the course, there was one family just ahead of one of our teams that consisted of a mum, dad and young girl of about nine years old. The way this amazing family worked as a team was inspiring. The little girl was a strong character but she was very scared at times, even to the point of shedding a few tears. Mum and dad were fantastic. They didn't bully her or push her into going ahead. Instead they encouraged her to not give up and with support and patience they encouraged her to keep going. They guided her through each obstacle with mum in front and dad behind her. This family stood out to me and I really admired them as they didn't overprotect their young daughter, nor did they push her too far; rather they talked her through every step in a gentle manner whilst speaking confidence into her so she could succeed.

They knew that there was no way she could hurt herself as the safety equipment was in place. They weren't making her do something she didn't want to do; they just took her through the whole process and set her up for victory. She was amazing and an inspiration too; she was scared at times but still didn't want to give up as she badly wanted to finish the course. The ingredients for her success were simple: a very supportive mum and dad who were willing to let this little girl work through the uncomfortableness with patience, kindness and gentleness. As parents finding that fine line that allows us to teach, not push too hard yet know when our children need to be encouraged to step out of their comfort zones, is challenging indeed. In order to understand that, I believe we as parents need that experience of pushing through our fears because, let's be honest, we all have something we are scared of. So, allowing them to see us take steps like this is invaluable for their own walk. If as parents we protect them too much, they will never have the opportunity to develop perseverance, persistence and that feeling of 'I conquered a mountain' so to speak.

> *We all need to face a mountain and begin to walk towards it with confidence*

If there is no cheer squad by your side then allow yourself to cheer you all the way. Or better yet, find someone in your life who will cheer you on as you endeavour to bring change to your world and to those around you.

Your mountain doesn't have to be climbing trees or jumping through obstacle courses, it may very well be public speaking, paddle boarding, the ocean, skateboarding, spiders or having people over for dinner. The list goes on. For me, I have decided that I want to take our whole family (all 22 of us) to TreeTops and have a go. I realise it will be challenging, that there could be tears, sweat and anxiety and I know that I personally won't like the journey, but I will love the destination.

Another example of stepping out of your comfort zone to overcome fear is Rob's story.

He moved from a very comfortable career and lifestyle to begin a new career in his fifties.

Rob had worked for an amazing boss, Ken Jolly, for a company that had looked after him very well for over twenty years. However, there came a time in Rob's life when he wanted to step out on his own and create a business that not only supported him financially but also made a difference in this world. And so, in his fifties when most people are preparing to slow down in life, preparing for retirement, Rob stepped up and out to create Little Miracles.

Little Miracles has over the years become our family business; all of our four adult children perform key roles within the company.

At the time Rob stepped out of his comfort zone, there were many people who thought he was taking too big a risk at that stage of life, however he believed it was what he was meant to do and so the adventure began.

There have been many challenges along the way. Rob had to learn a whole new business model; fortunately he had a background in finance and so he could apply those same principals in his new business.

The first four years were very tough going; it was an extremely steep learning curve for Rob learning all the ins and outs of Early Childhood which are very involved and challenging. Rob has created a company that is setting children up to thrive in life by stepping out and overcoming fears and the many obstacles along the way.

If Rob hadn't taken his fears on and learnt how to overcome them one by one, Little Miracles wouldn't exist and lives wouldn't be impacted as they are right now. Little Miracles equips not only the children to reach their full potential, but we also empower and equip our precious Educators.

Whenever we want to accomplish things in life there will always be fears to overcome; I could write another whole book on all the fears Rob has had to overcome to create Little Miracles. Never let your fears or the fears of others stop you from stepping out. You can do it; you can overcome your fears.

When our children were young we used to sing a song about how you climb a mountain one step at a time. That's how life is done, one fear at a time.

F alse
E xpectations
A ppearing
R eal.

That's all fear is, you can overcome.

May we all be parents who always cheer our children and grandchildren on to be free to not only face their fears, but to conquer them through our belief in them and allowing them to see us as we bravely and fearlessly face and conquer our own fears.

Identity

Today you are you
That is truer than true
There is no one alive
Who is youer than you.

Dr Seuss

My Self-Esteem And Its Effect On My Children

As a mother of adult children, I have become very aware of how the self-esteem of both Rob and myself has had an effect on our children and now our grandchildren. Hindsight, being 20:20, has given me a unique perspective, allowing me the opportunity to look back and see how, even as a young parent, our self-esteem played a huge role.

Our confidence in our identity and knowing who we are **automatically transfers onto our children.** This way of being, of knowing and living provides a strong foundation for our children and one that they can springboard off of, helping them create a strong identity of their own.

The opposite is also true – insecurity and lack of confidence also affects our children. They are often a reflection of our true self. Previously I spoke about 'Monkey See, Monkey Do'. Our actions, our words and the way we live out of our sense of identity impacts those around us.

As a parent today, one of the greatest conversations I have with my children is about identity and hearing them talk about how Rob and I walked in the confidence of who we were and how that impacted them. Knowing that we were secure in ourselves and speaking that into our children, produced confidence, life and freedom for them to walk in.

As you are reading this and (perhaps) thinking, "Great Susanna, glad you made all this happen and you helped your kids in this area, but I'm failing miserably," can I stress that we aren't and never have been perfect parents. We have made our fair share of mistakes along the way and I'm thankful for forgiveness, second chances and the understanding that tomorrow is another day. Here's the thing – you don't have to be perfect parents to produce great children. Gosh! Imagine if that were a prerequisite – we'd all be in big trouble!

> *Here's the thing – you don't have to be perfect parents to produce great children.*

When talking to my children I love hearing about the different situations they have found themselves in and still find themselves in. I am grateful that they have found encouragement by observing Rob and I as we have walked through our challenges remaining confident of great outcomes simply because we have known who we are and why we are here.

We all know that life is not (always) a bed of roses. We all have challenges every day, week, month and sometimes years. What I have discovered, through it all, is that when we meet our challenges with a strong foundation of a healthy identity, the challenges are much easier to work through and the results always look better. None of us were created to live a life with limitations that hold us back and find us wishing our lives could be different. We are meant to understand our value and worth and live a life full of hope and dreams for ourselves and our children, confident that our future is secure.

Regardless of your past, I would like to remind you that you are extremely valuable and the value that was placed into and over you at your conception and that was realised at your birth cannot increase or decrease.

YOU ARE YOU AND YOU ARE WONDERFULLY UNIQUE.

You were born full of potential, value and worth. Sadly, as we journey through life we can get knocked about, our identity can shake and we can begin to doubt our worth and start to have low self-esteem. Thankfully, self-esteem has been something I have nurtured over the years. Like many of you, 'life' has happened to me and I have had to cultivate this strong knowing of who I am. I have had to learn how to stay strong, to remain confident and to walk in the fullness of who I have been created to be. I would like to encourage you to do the same. Life is a journey not a destination and we are all continually growing in this as life goes on. We have a choice – as life goes on we can either grow more and more confident of who we are or less and less so. We need to be deliberate and intentional as we build strong awareness within ourselves because if we don't others will give us their opinions and we will believe lies instead of the truth.

You were created to be loved, to receive love and to give love. Understanding your identity and realising how special you are places you in a position to truly receive and to give love in a healthy way. Over the next few chapters I will share more on this. I hope you will stick with the conversation as I share openly and honestly, all in an effort to help you see how amazing you are. Once you get a revelation of that, you will see your life change and the positive impact you will have on your children will go from strength to strength. I look forward to empowering you to be the best version of you that you are designed to be.

As A Person Thinks, So Is He Or She

As I said before, I believe we need to be deliberate in building a strong, healthy, self-esteem for ourselves so that we can pass it on to our children.

I recently heard an urban myth that I want to share with you. It goes like this:

Once there was a pregnant dog that was hit by a car and sadly, her back legs were broken. She received treatment but she was unable to walk properly again after the accident; she could only drag her back legs behind her as she walked. When her puppies were born they were completely normal but when they learnt to walk, they too dragged their legs behind them, just like their mum. They did this even though their legs were strong and healthy.

As parents, we need to make sure we don't drag our back legs when it comes to our confidence and self-esteem because our children catch more than they are taught. Our self-esteem is created in our minds, it goes into our spirits and out through our response to what we believe about ourselves. This then, is lived out in our actions and our words. So, our mind needs to be full of healthy thoughts about ourselves. As Australians we often criticise people who are sure of themselves. We seem to be intimidated by this confidence yet, if we aren't confident in who we are we can never become who we were created to be. Here lies the tension that needs to be solved by each one of us; a personal journey, indeed.

I want us all to know and understand that **being confident in ourselves is not arrogance**; rather it is being responsible with the potential we have been entrusted and blessed with. Arrogance comes when we feel we are better than others, confidence and healthy self-esteem helps us appreciate ourselves and when we operate from that place, we are better equipped to appreciate others and cheer them on.

How do we develop and grow self-esteem and confidence?

First and foremost, it begins in our mind and with our thought life. I believe it all starts with a thought and thankfully, our thoughts can be controlled and like any kind of training program or even diet, we need to be aware of what we are feeding on and letting into our minds. We need to feed our mind with healthy thoughts, and we need to exercise our brain to begin to believe those thoughts. Science has proven that a healthy thought life creates not only healthy self-esteem but also healthy bodies.

For many years now and with much practice and determination, Rob and I have guarded (very jealously, I might add) our thought life. After doing this I can assure you that it is imperative and absolutely necessary to know and check what you have your mind focused on. It is well known that your words will always reflect what you are thinking.

> *Out of our mouth comes the overflow of what's in our heart and our mind.*

What our minds are feasting on is translated through our lips and can be heard loud and clear. If you are thinking thoughts that will build your confidence your will be speaking positively about yourself. If not, there will be a lot of down talk and self-doubt; equally there is probably some competitive thinking going on. I urge you, whenever you find yourself putting yourself down, check your thought patterns.

Additionally, Rob and I deliberately read books and listen to speakers that inspire us to build our self-esteem. We put ourselves around people who have healthy self-esteem and speak well of themselves and others. There are lots of great books out there; grab hold of some and soak in them.

Another space that speaks to my self-esteem and a deep understanding of who I am as a woman of faith comes from God's word, the Bible. I love soaking in what God says about all of us and I make it personal to me. For example, things I speak to myself are: "I am His masterpiece", "I am fearfully and wonderfully made", "I have a future and a hope and peace", "I am altogether beautiful" and so much more richness within the text that speaks not only to my mind, but to my heart and soul, resulting in self-esteem with clarity.

I also love to read about other people's journeys and how they have learned to cultivate a healthy self-esteem for themselves.

I encourage you to be diligent in recognising any negative thought you have about yourself. You will need to delete it and replace it with the opposite. Why not find a quiet place and write out a list of all the things you like about yourself and make it as long as you like. If you have trouble finding something to write, don't worry about starting with big things, just start with small things. Appreciate them and your list will grow. If you are still really struggling, start with the fact that you produced your precious child. That in itself is a huge thing to celebrate about you and your value. If it weren't for you, they wouldn't be here.

Once you've written your list, celebrate all that you have written and start to really value these things about yourself. Then, every day this week, remind yourself about what you like about yourself and keep adding to your list when other things come to your mind. I promise, you will be surprised what a great person you are and how much value you truly have.

Who Do You Want To Be?

As we travel through this conversation of identity and self-esteem, I've been thinking about our conversations with our little ones. I remember asking my kids the question "What do you want to be when you grow up? A fireman, a doctor, a builder?" We all do this; we all ask what it is we want to do. As our children go through school, this question remains. When they hit their final years of school the question is amplified and as parents if this decision hasn't been made, we grow concerned.

This question is interesting because we have dreams for our children and that's okay. When they first enter our world, we watch them catch or kick balls, dancing or singing, painting and drawing and we wonder. We wonder what the future will hold and what will they do.

> *You is smart, you is kind and you is important.*

Allow me to shift the conversation. I quickly learned that although what they do (in life) is important, the more important question is "Who do you want to be?" This question allows us the opportunity to speak life into their character, into the core of their being. When our children are little we can ask the question and help them by answering, "You (insert your child's name here) are kind, you are good and you are smart." Yes, I realise that this sounds a lot like the famous line from the movie *The Help* where the gorgeous Aibileen constantly reminds wee Mae Mobley that, "You is smart, you is kind and you is important." In this movie Aibileen shows how **we are able to speak life into a child's heart, mind and soul.** She recites the same sentence to the small child every day, repeatedly reminding her of her value and who she is. Because of this daily affirmation Mae Mobley is able to decide who she wants to be. Brilliant!! In this scene Aibileen not only says it to the little girl, but she masterfully gets Mae Mobley to speak it out loud to herself.

I hope this helps as you endeavour to help build self-esteem in your children. I know that it will impact your life in addition to your children's. It's amazing that when you begin to speak the truth about yourself, a beautiful confidence emerges and you begin to walk in a way that impacts others. In doing so, the truth of Marianne's Williamson's quote, which I shared in the very first chapter, opens up the door for you to give others permission to do the same.

I wonder, "Who do YOU want to be?"

How Do You Want To Get There?

Now that you have thought about 'Who You Want to Be', how about we start thinking about 'How You Want to Get There'. Becoming the person you are meant to be is a journey and it starts with simply BEing; being you, the best version of you that you can be.

That may sound easy but I can assure you, and I'm sure some of you would agree, it is challenging at times. Being a great version of yourself often times means walking in the opposite direction to where your heart, mind or maybe even your temperament wants you to go. It's taking time to relax into yourself and finding the space to allow you to get to know yourself. Did you know that most people don't allow time to really get to know themselves? It's true and we all need to find out what we like, what we don't like, what colours, or even food, we like; what music moves us, how art impacts us and how others impact us. Sadly, because we don't do this, many people begin to believe things about themselves simply because someone once said something about them or to them.

I once heard a story about a young boy in Year 3 who loved to sing. He loved his music class and looked forward to it every week. On one particular day, his teacher decided to tell him that he couldn't sing and that he sounded awful. Now, was the teacher in a particularly bad mood that day? Did she have a flat tyre on the way to work or perhaps a morning fight with her partner? Who knows what happened that day to cause that teacher to say such a thing. The result of her saying those cruel words was that that young boy is now a grown man with teenage daughters and he never sang again. In his adult years, he attends church regularly yet, during the singing/worship time, he simply mouths the words or shifts from side to side. You see, he believed what was said about him and it held him back and changed something deep inside him. Who knows, he could have been the next great singer of our time. Alas, we will never know.

That story saddens me. Yes, we can write it off, make excuses and explain away how that little boy could have walked over those words. It's true he could have, but he didn't.

My point, and the reason I share it, is to say that in order to become who we want to be we have to get there. As I said in the beginning of this chapter the 'getting there' is the hard part. It means silencing the voices around you and daring to walk into the unknown. It means not following the crowd but blazing a new trail. It may mean taking a few risks and trusting that 'still small voice' that you can hear from within. It means taking time to pause and **let your core breathe and stand up on the inside**. It means taking steps every day towards the goal of 'who you want to be'. The steps might be scary and challenging but taking them and 'doing it scared', knowing that the outcome is worth it, is what it's all about.

Over my lifetime I have stopped at different points on the journey to reassess who I am, who I want to be and what I need to do to get there.

In my mid-forties I came to a place of realising I had to be set free of a huge phobia that had plagued me since childhood. If I was going to live my life true to who I wanted to be I had to make a very difficult decision and have a complete change of mindset.

Snakes!! A phobia about snakes was holding me back; I was totally paralysed when it came to even think about snakes. As a small child I had regular nightmares about them killing my parents and the fear it instilled in me grew and grew until I was totally overwhelmed at just the thought of snakes. I would never let my children eat lolly snakes; if there was a book with snakes in it I could not bear to touch it. We were living on acreage at the time and when you live in Australia you can be certain that if you have paddocks for cows and horses you will probably have snakes around, which we did. I knew that not only was I not living to my full potential, but I was also creating fear in my children.

This was all very out of character for me as I am usually a confident person and not much stops me. Something had to happen and I knew that something wasn't going to be easy but very necessary if I was to get to where I was created to be. After praying about what I needed to do to overcome this phobia and to show my children how we are all meant to live in complete freedom, I knew what I had to do.

Near where we live there is a Reptile Park where visitors can view and, in some cases, mingle with native animals including snakes. Up until this time I had never been to the Park; a close girlfriend of mine had taken my children but I couldn't bring myself to walk through the gates knowing there were snakes inside the Park. Now I knew I had to go and view the snakes.

Michael, our third child, was about fourteen at the time and he had a friend called Luke who was madly in love with snakes. Luke was a year older than Michael and I knew if I was to go to this Park I had to have someone with me who had no fear at all of snakes. After asking Luke to help me overcome my fear, he and I set out to go and visit the snake enclosure where the snake handler walks around with the snakes and each person has an opportunity to pat the snake as he teaches you all about them. Luke and I were standing at the enclosure amongst the crowd who were all I very interested. I was shaking all over! I took a deep breath and to my and Luke's surprise I didn't turn and run away when the handler and his snake passed us by. I was so proud of myself and Luke was amazing, encouraging me all the way. Then Luke suggested I stay where I was right at the fence of the enclosure and try and pat the snake next time around. I was really scared, not wanting to touch that snake and totally freaking out.

Then I stopped myself; looking around I saw that everyone who patted the snake was just fine. I took another deep breath and said to myself, 'I can do this; I need to do this to be free'. As the snake came around, with encouragement from Luke, I reached out and stroked the snake, making sure it was very quick and I was nowhere near its head. It was so amazing; I felt a freedom come over me. I was totally free of my phobia!

I still have a healthy respect of snakes and have never patted one again; however my phobia left me that day. I am pleased to say that my children were then allowed to have lolly snakes and I eat them myself - always from the head first just to remind myself how good it feels to be free.

I encourage you to take some time and really reflect on your own life and who you want to be and how you want to get there. Be brave enough to change what needs to be changed and to embrace what needs embracing. As you do this, look at your children and see how you can influence their walk of freedom. Free to be the best versions of themselves they can be.

What an extraordinary place to live from.

Words

Words are containers for power;
you choose what kind of power
they carry.

Joyce Meyer

The Power Of The Spoken Word

I'm a big believer in 'Speaking Life' to those in my sphere of influence. I believe that the spoken word has power and that **there is the power of life and death in the tongue**.

Does this sound a little harsh and 'out there'? Well, believe me, I know, like all of you know (personally) how words can hurt and equally, how they can heal.

I find myself thinking about that age old saying, 'Sticks and stones can break my bones, but words will never hurt me'. I'm not sure who came up with that, but what a load of rubbish the second part of that saying is – the 'words will never hurt me' part.

I challenge you to take a moment to think about your week. Think about the words that have been spoken to you, around you and maybe you've even heard some that have been said behind your back. Maybe one of your little ones used some choice words to express their emotion to you or about you; if you have older ones this is probably more relevant.

Nevertheless, think about the words that you have heard this week and explore how they made you feel. If they were kind and encouraging words, you probably feel on top of the world and ready to take on any challenge or you're simply smiling because you feel good about yourself and that's great! On the other hand, if they were words that hurt or perhaps discouraging, then you are probably left feeling quite flat, out of steam and even a little angry.

You see, words affect us in so many ways. Not only do they affect the way we feel, but they can affect us long term; especially if we hear them repeatedly or we go over and over them in our mind, reminding ourselves of what someone said. Eventually we *could* begin to believe them and at times they become self-fulfilling prophecies and we don't even realise what's happening.

Now I want you to think about your children. How often have they come home saying 'so-and-so called me this' or, 'they said this about me'. The list goes on. Simply put, your child has heard words spoken that have hurt rather than healed. Now, think about the days they have come home telling you about how the teacher pointed their artwork out or how well they listened during reading or craft. Or maybe a special friend told them they were their best friend; on these days they run, they smile, they bounce and they are happy.

Words have power.

Remember the story about the ten-year-old boy who liked to sing but hasn't sung a note for 40 years because of hurtful, discouraging words spoken to him by his bad-tempered music teacher?

His teacher didn't choose words that would build and encourage him; rather she used words that put him and his love for music in a box with a lid. From that day on, the little boy turned down his volume and he has never been able to enjoy music again. The words she spoke to a ten-year-old boy have echoed in his mind for 40 years and sadly, the music that played so loudly within this vibrant, eager ten-year-old, shut down that day. Steve was silenced by words.

Lisa Nichols' high school English teacher once said Lisa was the weakest writer she had ever met in her entire life. She is now a *New York Times* bestselling author of seven books. The same year her speech teacher recommended she never speak in public. She is now a world-renowned motivational speaker.

Imagine that – someone telling you that you can't do something that you know you can.

NEVER DIM YOUR LIGHT FOR THE SAKE OF OTHERS. IN FACT, MAKE IT BRIGHTER.

This is a perfect message to teach your kids, but first teach yourself. I love this kind of success story – seeing Lisa's cheeky smile because she did exactly what someone told her she could never do.

Lisa says, "I want you to remember that your 70 watts has to be turned up, because you've got way more to give us; it ain't over yet. And when you've turned it up to 159 watts you know you keep turning it up. There will always be people on the lookout for souls to speak lies to, to hurt people so that they are afraid to be who they are. Fear is not your friend. It darkens your spirit. Find that spark that is only yours and let no one put it out before it has even turned into a flame. **There's a fire in everyone's heart.** Please, friends, do not be the one with the extinguisher."

Lisa talks about these people with a humour which I love because she realises how little they contribute to her life. Instead of dwelling on the negatives, she embraces them, she calls us to forgive the unforgivable, love the unlovable and pray for those who hurt us instead of being angry at them. You are just wasting precious energy on them, energy that could be used so much better searching for the next best big breakthrough in your life.

"You gonna find people that can't handle your light… Turn the lights up, as your light gets brighter, you gonna disrupt some people. Then you just look at them and say, 'I'm not dimming my light – I'm just gonna hand you some shades.'" – Lisa Nichols.

Speak Life to one another and into your homes and you will be amazed at the fruit.

As you think about your words, also think about the fact that children are like sponges; they absorb absolutely everything. If that is true, then what words are they absorbing that have been spoken to them and over them? I'm not asking this to make you feel bad or to bring any sort of condemnation; rather I want you to think about it because I believe it's imperative that we speak life into and over our children. Words can heal, words can encourage, and words can build.

Here's an example:

"Lucas, you never clean your room and it's always a mess."
"Lucas, I love it when your room is clean and how it makes you feel."

I realise that this example is simple but let me expand. The first statement is just that, a statement, and an end to any conversation or the beginning of a confrontation. The second is uplifting and creates space for growth and inspiration. There are so many more examples I could use but I think you get where I'm going with this.

Our children hear so many negative words in their world, whether it is through media, things others say or perhaps their own voice rehashing things that have been said. With that in mind, let's replace those words with words of life that breathe vision, dreams and hopes within their little and oh so precious hearts. Let's use words that encourage conversation and discussion, instead of shutting it down. I promise you will be amazed at how they respond when you begin to speak life into and over those people in your world.

Masaru Emoto, a Japanese author and entrepreneur, claims that human consciousness has an effect on the molecular structure of water. Emoto's hypothesis has evolved over the years. Initially, he believed that water takes on the 'resonance' of the energy which is directed at it, and that polluted water can be restored through prayer and positive visualisation. Emoto's work is widely considered to be pseudoscience, yet his findings and subsequent experiments by many others seem to show some meaning.

Since 1999 Emoto has published several volumes of a work titled *Messages from Water*, which contains photographs of water crystals and their accompanying experiments. Emoto's ideas appeared in the documentary *What the Bleep Do We Know?* Feel free to Google the videos.

I am fascinated by the affect positive words and thoughts have on water and how the negative thoughts and words change the structure so much. The thing that stands out for me the most is when he talks about his findings and then talks about the human body. Being that we are about 60% water would suggest that positive and negative words must have an impact on us.

How do I work this theory in my own life? I choose to speak life into every situation. Whatever the circumstance or what lies in front of me, I choose my words wisely and I speak life into and over everything. I truly believe that by doing this **I am able to create a reality that is beyond what can be seen**. I choose words of life, healing, hope and love and those words are the foundation for every conversation in my life. Throughout my day I will often meditate (like Emoto mentions). For me, I meditate on scripture. One in particular that I like to focus my heart and mind on is found in the Book of Romans. The scripture is Romans 8:28: 'And we know that in all things God works for the good of those who love him, who have been called according to his purpose.'

Fathers, I encourage you to speak highly of your children. Encourage them and breathe life into them through your words – your sons and daughters need to hear you believing in them. Mothers, your words comfort, heal and bring peace into a home, so I implore you to use your words wisely.

I really hope this helps and that you are able to practically work this out in your life. From my experience, I can tell you that you will not only see, but you will also feel a tangible difference.

Once again, I say "Go for it!"

Laughter Is The Best Medicine

As I've been sharing my thoughts with you about the power of words I've been reminded about laughter and how important it is to have laughter in our homes.

I know for Rob and I, laughter has been a big part of our 47 years together. Trust me, you don't get to 47 years of marriage and not learn to laugh at yourself and at times at each other. Also, when I hear my grandchildren laughing it automatically brings joy in my heart and puts a smile on my face. It gives me a real sense of freedom and a light heart like nothing else can. I can literally feel my spirit rise and I am energised by it and I feel love filling my heart. **I find laughter to be very powerful**. Actually, I have been rather unwell lately (that nasty flu that goes around every year has found me…). While I have been sick and have been spending most of my time on the couch, I hear my grandchildren, who are living downstairs, enjoying a laugh together every now and then and it's like life and healing itself being released into my spirit and body. Oh, what a feeling!

When older people are asked about how they stay so young or remain in good health or when you read articles on the subject, laughter will often emerge as the reason. I recently read a claim that states that children laugh more frequently than adults do. In fact, the numbers thrown around are that children laugh more than 300 times a day, whereas adults laugh less than 20 times a day. Now that says something.

I have a young friend who has three children and she says one of her favourite sounds is the sound of her children's laughter echoing through the house. I often think how nice that is. She loves the sound of her children laughing and carrying on. I think about those numbers recorded about laughter and the vast difference between children and adults. I understand that as we age, stress creeps in and much of our innocent joy can be taken or even erased.

I've heard it said and I agree with this statement, 'Don't let anyone steal your joy.' As I consider laughter and it being good medicine, I think about how important it is that we protect our joy; that **joy can be our strength**. I know, for myself, being a woman of faith and trusting God, I adhere to a Scripture that says, 'The joy of the Lord is your strength.' This brings me great courage to protect my joy, to hold on to it and to know that joy is strength. As I think about this I'm also reminded of that line in *The Lion King* where Simba says, "Ha, I laugh in the face of danger." It's a line that has resonated with me because as I have travelled through life I realise that stressful times will come, that challenges can be scary and that fear can creep in to the recesses of our hearts, however, like Simba, I have chosen to laugh in the face of danger. I choose to let joy rise and my circumstances be shaken.

Sometimes, however, it's hard to find joy again when circumstances steal it away and we need help to find it again. For me, I find that immersing myself in something beautiful for a while restores my joy. By sitting for a while in whatever we find beautiful, somehow makes us happy and restores joy to our hearts in unexpected ways.

In a statistical analysis of happiness done by Abraham Goldberg, a professor at the University of South Carolina Upstate, and his team it was found that happiness was coming from an unexpected place. It was found that people living in aesthetically beautiful cities were the happiest. 'The cumulative positive effects of daily beauty works subtly but strongly'. It was recorded that moments where people recorded the highest levels of happiness were all related to beauty.

So if you need to have your joy restored immerse yourself in something you find beautiful; it could be a walk on the beach or in the bush, watching a feel good movie, a visit to an art gallery or a museum, listening to your favourite music or it could just be watching your children play.

I trust all of this makes sense to you and I hope that wherever you find yourself today and whatever you are facing, you can find joy in the midst of it. Remember, sometimes we need to take a step back and allow joy to invade our space once again. If that's you then take the step, relax and let joy take over.

I encourage you to **let laughter find its place in your homes and your hearts**. Choose to find something to laugh about, find a joke, have a food fight, throw some water balloons, play twister or a funny game of charades or maybe watch a funny movie. Whatever it is, find something that makes you laugh and remember, laughter is infectious so once you start, be ready for your home to be filled with the beauty of joy.

Inspiring Quotes For Kids

As I close this section on the power of words, whether spoken, written or even words that we think, to heal, hurt, harm, build, inspire or motivate, I thought I would leave you with some quotes that you can take, make your own and use them to inspire your children to live strong, confident, happy lives. Cut and past them and use them everywhere. Make signs that you can stick on walls, doors, mirrors and fridges so that they can serve as a reminder each and every day. Love one another and allow the words to speak life into the lives around you.

Words are powerful and used correctly, they can make life better in an instant.

Why fit in when you can stand out. – Dr Seuss

Be yourself. Everyone else is already taken. – Oscar Wilde

You will never influence the world by trying to be like it. – Unknown

Sometimes the smallest things take up the most room in your heart. – Piglet

It's a very cool thing to be a smart girl. – Unknown

Kindness is a language that the deaf can hear and the blind can see. – Mark Twain

Be silly, be honest, be kind. – Ralph Waldo Emerson

How lucky am I to have something that makes saying goodbye so hard. – Winnie the Pooh

If you have good thoughts they will shine out of your face like sunbeams and you will always look lovely. – Roald Dahl

Never give up on what you really want to do. The person with big dreams is more powerful than one with all the facts. – Albert Einstein

Winning doesn't always mean being first. Winning means you're doing better than you've done before. – Bonnie Blair

You're braver than you believe, and stronger than you seem, and smarter than you think. – A.A. Milne/Christopher Robin

In any moment of decision, the best thing you can do is the right thing. The worst thing you can do is nothing. – Theodore Roosevelt

All your dreams can come true if you have the courage to pursue them. – Walt Disney

Raising Kids In An Age Of Technology

> *Yes, kids love technology, but they also love Legos, scented markers, handstands, books and mud puddles. It's all about balance.*
>
> **K.G. First grade teacher**

Keeping Our Children Safe In A Technological World

Our world is crowded with technology. **We are fighting for face time** (and I don't mean via the iPhone). As parents and grandparents, we find ourselves in a world where our kids are captivated more by what is on screens than what is right before them – real life.

Whether its games or the constant texting between tweens and teens or even movie watching, we are fighting for time and space with an ever-changing world that has the ability to take our children on a journey that doesn't include us.

I raised my children before any of this existed, which gives me the opportunity to form an opinion based on what I have not only seen but experienced both as a parent, grandparent and care provider.

Now, I understand what technology provides in terms of assistance when you are out shopping or in the car traveling or perhaps watching an older sibling's Saturday sports. Maybe you use it when you are at the hairdressers and babysitters are few and far between. Gosh, I would have loved to have had something to keep my little ones captivated, even for a moment, so that I could relax and enjoy a cuppa.

We use technology to teach the children in Little Miracles Childcare and Pre School centres and we have created our own app to teach children to read. Technology is a wonderful and powerful tool for our children and their futures. It's like anything, it just needs to be used well.

We need to create healthy boundaries when it comes to technology. The challenge comes when we let the boundary lines slip. Have your boundaries slipped or are you yet to create them to keep your children safe?

If you have set your boundaries, GREAT! Well done. If you haven't, don't worry, but start now. If they've slipped, that's okay too, let's just get back on track.

What do these boundaries look like and why should you create them? First let's look at why we should create them:

1. Research shows that kids who have more screen time struggle with obesity and attention problems.
2. Anger issues tend to arise, especially within boys, due to the constant stimulation and frustration with real life.
3. Personal connectivity gets lost and isolation becomes more comfortable and normal.
4. Online personas become all-consuming and more engaging than real life.
5. Online bullying typically takes place between 8 pm and the early morning hours. This may not seem relevant to you and your toddler, however keep in mind, you are creating habits that will take them into their tween and teen years. You need to create boundaries and establish them now.

These are just five simple reasons why we should be creating HEALTHY boundaries around technology. Now, the big step – I would like to give you some pointers on how you create healthy boundaries:

1. Decide when and why you are using technology to help your day.

2. Determine how long a period of time your child can use technology. Use an egg timer or the timer on your phone so they know that when the timer goes, technology ceases.

3. Turn off all technology at meal times and create a healthy face-to-face zone that will mean a lot when your children are teens… trust me on this one!

4. NO TECHNOLOGY IN PRIVATE SPACES. By this I mean, nothing in bedrooms or quiet corners away from the eye of a parent.

5. Parental Controls are a MUST. Put them on and if you don't know how, do some research and find out how you can monitor not only their activity but their time spent online.

6. Choose a time to TURN IT OFF. Decide what hour of the day you will unplug your modem, thus restricting online access throughout your house. Now this may sound strange and tough but again, trust me, it's so worth it and so good. This will help create conversation and draw your family together.

7. Find alternative things to do as a family: go for a hike (especially when the weather is beautiful), bake something, involve your children in dinner prep (set the table, toss the salad, etc.), get them to help fold the laundry (towels are perfect for this, especially tea towels).

I encourage you to set your boundaries and do the 'hard yards' now as you will reap the benefits not only now, but in the years to come. Use of technology is only increasing and demanding more of our waking hours. **It is incumbent upon all of us to keep our children safe** not only from those lurking in forums and masquerading as gamers, but from losing all their time and missing out on what truly matters…. Real Life.

What Are Your Kids Watching And Hearing?

Let's talk about the power of words in the context of technology.

As I've been thinking about this in context of these articles, I've also been thinking about the things our kids see and hear outside of our conversations with them. With gaming stations, social media and looser restrictions on television, I am shocked at the content that our babes are being exposed to at such young ages.

Whether it's the level of violence on the Xbox or PlayStation or the ads that come on TV during the 'non-primetime' hours, or perhaps it's as simple as the news reports on the drive to school, our kids are seeing and hearing things that trouble their little souls. Constant shooting, yelling and profanities that plague the online games they play, or even hearing about the latest airline disasters, it's little wonder they are stressed and start acting out when we take them on what should be fun family getaways.

Stress, anxiety and other nervous system challenges are just a few of the most common problems for children right now. I can't help but think it has something to do with the constant bombardment of inappropriate viewing and hearing.

My suggestion is simple. I strongly encourage you to engage with your children when it comes to their viewing pleasure. Even if it's as innocent as watching TV before bedtime, engage with them and know what is landing on them. When it lands on them, they have to do something with it; they have to process it in some way. Children aren't able to process most of what is handed to them. They are dealing with adult issues and it is incumbent upon us that we help them by protecting their eyes, ears and hearts.

I hope this helps and I encourage you to know what your kids are watching and hearing because with knowledge you can lead and you can teach.

What Are You Letting In?

We've been talking about boundaries and I find this subject quite interesting. Boundaries define our lives. Whether it be the land we own, the state we live in or the sports we play, boundaries define the parameters in which we can operate.

Boundaries provide distinct guidelines providing structure. Boundaries are lines that cannot be broken and that must be adhered to. As I've mentioned before, **setting boundaries for my children was a great way to teach them along the road to independence.** I loved watching the boundary lines expand and their little lives grow with them.

Today, I'd like to focus more on the boundaries that we, as parents, put in place. Recently, I was having coffee with a young friend of mine and she was telling me about a television show she watched. She had heard a lot about this show, which I've come to learn is a very popular series and has captivated many couples. I was interested to learn what my friend thought about this series.

My friend decided to sit down and watch the show and was surprised at what she discovered. Now, I don't want to go into much of the detail regarding the show as I prefer not to give much airtime to things that fall outside of my personal boundary lines. However, for the purpose of this article I understand I need to provide context. What my friend quickly learned was that this particular series was nothing more than explicit material being shared on TV; another opportunity to push individual boundaries in terms of what is appropriate during primetime television. The show did have an impact on her, as after watching it, she decided that there were areas of her life that she decided were 'boring'. Did the show help her or did it encourage her to push her boundary lines out and step into spaces that she had promised never to tread?

She came to the conclusion that she had (indeed) gone into a space that was previously off-limits and now had the task of pulling the tent pegs back and re-establishing her boundary lines.

I share this with you today simply to ask the question: 'What are you letting in?' Understanding that we are body, soul and spirit and we need to manage and protect all three, it's important to realise that we can open up areas of our lives and in doing so, we run the risk of things 'sticking' to us. Perhaps what we've let in may cause us to weaken our resolve in specific areas of our lives.

What are you letting in? What are you watching, listening to and even reading? Protect yourself and feed on healthy things that will minister and speak to your body, soul and spirit. Take time to find words or music that soothe you and create some quiet time for you. There are so many beautiful ways for you to rest and think of beauty and peace such as in nature, music, art, poetry, etc. In my case, I love to find a Bible verse that I can rest on and think through. I find great solace in prayer and often find my mind wandering through a list of people or things to pray about.

> *Let things in that will build you from the inside out.*

Choose to silence the whispers that encourage you to let the boundaries lines slip. When the urge comes and you are considering pushing the boundary lines out remember that you have tiny eyes and ears watching, listening and learning from you. Choose wisely what you let in.

Reading With Your Child

At Little Miracles we are passionate about reading and teaching children to read. We are committed to seeing children learn, not just to read, but to comprehend what it is they are reading. We try and establish a love for the written word.

In the world today we are bombarded with easy solutions to 'simplify' reading, our need to read and even how we read. Technology has helped this along and in some cases the solutions are useful, but sadly, many leave us almost wordless. The use of texting and using shortcuts seem to make life 'easier' and our communication much quicker. I have one friend who has resorted to using the letter K to respond to text messages that usually require an OK. I often wonder what she could possibly do with all that time she saves by eliminating the O in OK… Funny, I know. I love the written word and I understand how important it is that we not only teach our children, but we also learn to appreciate reading with them. I am passionate about encouraging parents to read with their children. It not only helps them and boosts their confidence but it allows you some much needed 'down-time' in this busy world we find ourselves in.

Reading with your children allows time and space for conversation to flow, whether it be about the book or perhaps the time spent together simply allows space for spoken words to grow and develop. I know that as a young mother, spending time buried in a book with my children created opportunities for conversation. Another thing reading with your children creates is the ability to escape. What do I mean by that?

> *Books and stories have the ability to take us into new places and spaces in our imagination.*

We become world travellers, explorers and adventurers. The written word offers an escape from our everyday lives which is at times a much-needed distraction. Whether it's been a tough day at work for you or maybe your child had a challenging day at school, reading can be a relaxing escape that renews and refreshes the soul.

Here are some things that I found helped foster healthy reading habits in my home:

- Lead by example. Let your children see you reading (remember, Monkey See, Monkey Do)
- Learn what your child likes to read and visit the library to borrow books.
- Create a healthy reading space. Perhaps a comfy chair, a bean bag or, if you like to cosy up in bed, make sure you have a great bedside table lamp.
- Use a bookshelf and begin to build up a family library
- Talk about what you are reading or have read, at the dinner table.
- Find 20 minutes/week and commit to a family reading time.

These are just a few ideas that will help you develop reading habits that will become part of their lives. Remember, everyone's reading habits are different. I have a friend with three children and they all love such different things. The eldest enjoys novels and always has; the middle child likes books on facts and history and the youngest child loves anything with humour. Three children from the same family but each one with such different interests.

Explore the world of books with your children and allow the written word to captivate them and to transport them into places they dream about. Spend time reading with them and engage with them. With your little ones, cuddle up in bed and find time to shut off all the outside distractions and enjoy your time together.

The written word is powerful. It can change lives, it can bring people together, it can challenge, motivate and inspire. It can cause people to dream and it can speak directly to the heart. **Words move us.** Enjoy reading with your children.

Teaching Kids To Listen

We all know how wonderful the minds of little children are – we love them dearly and are constantly fascinated by them.

The instant they are born we can see that their little minds begin to tick away. Thinking has begun, the world is at their fingertips and with every passing day more and more is explored by them. They communicate with us in such incredible ways; crying when hungry or sad, and giggling and smiling when they are happy. And then as they grow they learn to express further their thoughts in deeper ways. They begin to talk and can engage with us and share. And so, with their first breath of air, the process of *teaching them begins.*

Children echo and mimic everything we do and that's a large part of how they learn. When you stop to think about it, that's a HUGE responsibility and perhaps even a wake-up call. Our job is to teach them to use their words, to speak, and how to be heard, but there is something else we need to do and something I believe often gets neglected. We need to teach our children to listen to others, to one another, to their teachers and of course to us, their parents. Those are the obvious people they need to listen to, but what about teaching them to listen to themselves.

Do we spend much time teaching them to listen to that small voice within; to really be 'in touch' with themselves and to learn to trust their instinct, or what we also refer to as their conscience? Do we show them how to take time to quiet their hearts and their minds so that they can create space to listen? By doing this, **we really are giving them a gift that will travel with them throughout their life.**

For some of you reading this, you may be thinking that this is something you haven't even mastered yourself, so how on God's green earth are you going to teach your child to do this? Good question and if you haven't mastered the art of listening, don't worry... you aren't alone. Listening doesn't come easy to everyone and the world we live in doesn't really foster listening spaces. We are constantly entertained and are bombarded with information. We spend more time looking down at our devices and absorbing other people's images - for e.g. the walk they took, than appreciating the beauty of nature around us. It's funny how technology has changed so much. Our ears are constantly filled with white noise and space fillers. In fact, it would seem that the sound of silence has become something that can deafen us and is a foreign space for many.

I have a young friend who told me a story about her son who often speaks of his 'God Gut'. He says that whenever he is faced with a situation or circumstance that requires a decision or discernment or wisdom, he becomes very aware of his 'God Gut' and he does his best to rely on that. How beautiful that this young man is not only aware of this but has become reliant upon it. His mother was telling me that he has determined that 9/10 times his 'God Gut' is right and he needs to learn to listen more closely to it.

I love that story. I love that this young man has been encouraged by his parents to listen, to pause and to take heed of what is going on, on the inside of him. I think we can all learn from his 'God Gut'; whether you refer to it as conscience, intuition, a still small voice, or something else. *To listen is to learn and from a place of knowledge we can implement, act and live from a place that is in touch and awake.* We can teach very young children how to do this too. We just have to remember that their attention span is quite short. At Little Miracles we are aware that a child's attention span is usually determined by their age plus two. For example, if they are two years old, their attention span is maximised at four minutes; if they are three years old, it is maximised at five minutes. Don't' be put off by the fact that they can't sit still for long. You'll be surprised how they grow in this the more it's practiced.

We live in a beautiful world. Nature calls us into her lounge room – morning, noon and night. Why not accept the invitation and find yourself a seat on the sand, the grass or on one of our amazing bushwalks and **allow yourself the space to listen** and to practice the art of listening to the beauty that is around and in us. Let's take our children on this journey so that they too can learn the gentle art of listening.

In the next chapter we will dive a little deeper into some more practical ideas of how to listen, how to create space to do so, and more.

Teaching Kids How To Listen

Perhaps the first step on this journey of listening and teaching our children to listen is to first re-engage with it ourselves. It's so easy to get caught up in a world of white noise and forget what listening is about. Set a week aside for yourself and adopt a listening posture. Be intentional about putting your phone away, closing the computer and even forgoing time spent watching *My Kitchen Rules*, *Bachelor in Paradise* or your favourite Netflix series.

Find a quiet place in the house, maybe even light a candle and start by taking note of your breathing. Slow yourself down and sink into the world around you. Listen, and you'll be not only surprised at what you hear, but at how you feel.

As the week goes on, maybe even take some time to journal about your experience. Write down a list of the things you've heard and what you feel you could have missed. It could be as simple as the sound of the birds outside your kitchen window, the distant barking of a dog, the conversations your children have or the way your mother or a friend is speaking to you. All of a sudden words sound different, sentence structures tell a more in-depth story, nature calls and listening becomes an entirely new experience in your life.

After a week (or two if you're able or, more especially, if you've enjoyed your week so much that you want to take it further on your own first), suggest it to the family and make sure you start small. Every day, or every few days, add something new to the equation. Perhaps you can start at mealtimes, when outside distractions and devices are excluded from dinner. You might even need to clean off the dining room table so that you can eat together as a family.

A little later in the week you might suggest an after dinner walk and if it happens to be the weekend or school holidays, stretch it out and sit on the beach and watch the sunset or the twinkling of the night stars. I promise that these moments will be beneficial even if there is some opposition at the beginning. **It's like developing a new habit**; they say it takes seven days or longer to break the old and embrace the new. It's worth it, and you're not only benefiting yourself, but you're teaching your children a precious thing that they can take with them on their life's journey.

So as a **first step**: switch them off and step away.

Find a space for yourself and then help your kids to do the same. Make it a relaxing time and as a first step make sure distractions are removed. We are surrounded by beautiful beaches, national parks galore and just the serenity of nature everywhere. Even though quiet is hard to find, it is there if you look hard enough. Have you ever been to the beach at night and just listened to the waves? In the darkness, you can find quiet that stills the soul.

Then the **second step**: find a space.

The bushland in Australia is plentiful, even our cities have open spaces. Whatever time you can afford, 20 minutes or two hours – wander outside and listen to the wind in the trees and the birds and the wildlife. This is excellent family time, allowing us space to breathe and to be surrounded by the vast sky.

Let the soundtrack of nature alone and no other human voices be the calming start to your quiet time. Close your eyes in that chosen spot, breathe the fresh air in deep and learn the discipline and gentle art of listening. Make sure you practice this a few times before taking your kids with you.

When you take your children for a bush walk, help them see what is around them. Marvel at the wildflowers, stop and bend down and take time to see the beauty in the tiny things. Help your children take notice of the sun shining through the trees and look at the patterns it creates. Remind them to take note of the different variety of plants and then, when you get home, perhaps create a project around your wanderings. Maybe Google all the things they have found and learn how they are suited to that particular environment in which they are growing.

Then, ask them how they feel inside themselves when they are in the bush; how does it make them FEEL? As they answer even in the most simple, childlike manner help them explore and rest in that feeling so that they can begin to understand their own complex emotions. It doesn't have to be super deep and meaningful for them to begin the journey of listening to themselves and their environment.

If going outside is not possible for you, create a dedicated sanctuary in your own house. A beautiful friend of mine cleared a small space used for storage in a separate area of her home. She placed white sheets on the walls, laid a rug out, with cushions and minimal embellishments. It is a clear space away from the busyness and gives her clarity for her time to LISTEN.

The **third step** is: find your time.

To begin with – with the rush of every day, kid's routines, family arrangements, work and everything else in the mix, choosing a time seems daunting. It doesn't matter how long; it just matters that you choose.

Find time to breathe after you put your children to sleep, instead of watching the television sit in the dark and be at peace with yourself and your thoughts. Finding this time for yourself to listen is so important – it is so underestimated in our world where it seems we must be switched on and active every minute.

Finding a time like this with your kids is always a time to engage and grow with them. If you find yourself down at the beach playing with them, building sandcastles or going on a shell treasure hunt – ask them questions like: Why do you think the wave just knocked your castle down? How did that make you feel? What can we do about that feeling? How can we build it better and stronger for next time?

These types of questions help them regulate their feelings and emotions and they start to slowly learn how to listen to what's happening inside them and around them and they feel empowered and at peace.

At the dinner table, ask about their day and then go beyond what they did, by asking questions like "How did you feel when you did that?" or "How did it make you feel when that happened?" **Help them explore their feelings and emotions** so that they can learn to hear for themselves what's happening inside them.

Obviously, their answers won't be as deep as an adult's and nor should they be, they don't have the capacity for that.

This is just the beginning; you are just starting them on the journey of exploring how to listen, so don't expect too much, but be encouraged that you are making a huge difference to your child's ability to be confident within themselves and at peace with who they are.

Art and craft is another amazing way to stop and ask your child how they are feeling. Their art and craft often reflects what is happening internally.

Never assume you know what the painting or creation is all about; ask them open ended questions about it so they can express themselves and you will be surprised what you learn. Never, ever diminish any little thing they tell you; listen carefully to the answers and draw as much as you can out and then celebrate it with them.

There are so many more examples; reading with them before they go to bed is another way to teach them to listen. Try to not just read the book but explore with them what they think about the story and how it makes them feel. This expands their imaginations to think about being in the story, solving the problems and imagining themselves to be in new and 'fantastical' spaces.

> ***In your chaos, find your quiet.*** *It is there.*
>
> *In your busyness, find time to be still. It is there.*

Help your kids to do the same.

I hope this helps you and your family to breathe and listen to each other and to each individual's inner voice, grasping the beauty of the world around you and what God is trying to tell you. Oh that we could see the world with the eyes of a child – so filled with awe every day, crisp and bright and inquisitive. That is how we should listen to God.

Giving Back

We make a living by what we get. We make a life by what we give.

Winston S. Churchill

Teaching Our Children To Give Back

What does it mean to give back? How does one even begin to teach a child to give back? We all know how hard it is to settle a dispute between toddlers when one has taken a toy off the other and the tears begin to flow. Sadly, the injustices of life are felt at such tender ages. Even now, as adults, we struggle with the injustice that we see around us and at times we feel lost or even paralysed by the need that surrounds us. Where to begin seems like a mountain that is insurmountable.

Teaching our children to give back can be challenging and in the younger years, it is one of the big lessons we try and teach by sharing and caring for other's feelings. We remind them of what it felt like when they were in that position; we are constantly providing examples and helping them along the way. One of the things I've come to understand is that the old saying, 'Monkey See, Monkey Do' is very true. All you have to do is observe your child for long enough (as I'm sure many of you have done) and you marvel at the way he or she walks like you or your partner, how they have that same little wiggle. When they play dress-ups or play with their Barbies or action figures, you hear your words coming out in their stories. Why? Simply because these little eyes have been watching you, observing your every move and the words you use. You are the greatest influence in their young lives.

So, with that in mind, imagine now how you can teach them to give back. **You teach simply by doing** and sharing the experience with them through your words and your actions. You will be amazed at what you see in and through your amazing children as they learn from you in this manner.

I recently had the opportunity to be involved in a charity walk for an organisation called 'Hope Global'. Hope Global is a faith-based, non-profit organisation that operates to restore hope and justice to countries devastated by war, genocide and poverty. Their aim is to unite individuals, churches, governments, NGOs, education, trade, healthcare and business professionals to offer practical solutions that strengthen and help develop existing indigenous organisations. The primary objective of HOPE: Global is implement poverty reduction initiatives that achieve sustainable development and bring spiritual and social strength to every segment of society.

I love being involved in local initiatives that help our communities in Australia, but I also love being a part of something beyond our borders and the charity walk with Hope Global was just that; not only did we raise funds through our walk being sponsored but we made a strong statement saying, 'We will help, we will give back'. In addition to this, I am really excited to be taking our involvement with this charity a little further. My children and their families have been over to Rwanda to teach Early Childhood Teachers. They have a need and we are able to help so off we went, books and resources in hand and willing hearts to "Be the change we want to see in the world today" (Gandhi). Exciting days, for sure.

Even as a mother of grown children I was able to show them that no matter what your age, we should always be giving back. Once again, through the 'Monkey See, Monkey Do' principle my children and my grandchildren watched as I gave back of my time, my energy, my enthusiasm, my love and my heart for a world where injustice exists. Needless to say, I enjoyed the walk, the company and I look forward to the walk next year. What an opportunity and blessing.

There are local charities that help those in need in every city or town. Investigate and see how you and your family can help. It may be giving some toys or clothes away, or visiting elderly people who are isolated in their homes. Maybe you could help a neighbour or take food to the local shelter for the homeless or those in need. When children become aware of people's needs and learn that they can make a difference it creates gratitude and empowers them for life. Gratitude is so powerful.

I love it when my children and their children together meet the needs of underprivileged children and families in Bali through Bali Life Foundation and when they go to India and Rwanda. **In addition to helping people, this adds so much to their character.** It also makes my heart so proud when Little Miracles' educators go and volunteer their time and expertise in these places and when all our precious families help the educators provide such beautiful resources for them all.

So lovely families, let's continue to teach our children to give back. Let's show them how to do it by our example. Imagine a world where the thought of 'It's better to give than to receive' was a truth that was understood and lived out. What a world it would be.

The Importance Of Gratitude

Like many of you I have seen countless Facebook updates, Instagram posts, Tweets and even books written about gratitude. It seems to be a real focus as of late and for that I'm personally grateful.

As I have journeyed through life and experienced the different seasons, whether it be the early years of new love and marriage, the tired years of nappies, cracked nipples, nits and Saturday sport or the late nights waiting for teenagers to return home, or now as a doting grandmother, I have come to realise how important gratitude is and sometimes wish I had this revelation during those early years, the long days or the late nights.

You see, gratitude can take the focus off what you don't have or what frustrates you and creates the ability to see what you do have and what you enjoy in life. **Gratitude shifts our focus** and helps us hold onto hope and even a simple grateful thought can change us on the inside. When I find myself down in the dumps (so to speak) I try to find something, even the smallest of things to be grateful for (sometimes it's even the shoes on my feet or a gold coin in my wallet). It makes my insides jump. It's like there is a leap of faith and in an instant my focus has changed. I love that about gratitude.

I recently read something one of my dear friends, Darlene, wrote. Darlene was walking through breast cancer at the time and her words of gratitude were not only inspiring but challenging. She gets a lot of strength from her faith and her ability to share her journey is healing in many ways. Have a read from an excerpt that she wrote:

"Today, I wanted to say that although I would really rather this all be over, I DO know after 48 years, there are some things in life you just have to go THROUGH.

Psalm 23 reminds me daily that this is but a shadow. That this too shall pass and on the other side is a great party; truly a feast like no other. I rejoice by saying, "OH YES THERE WILL BE!!!""

He refreshes and restores my life (my self); He leads me in the paths of righteousness [uprightness] and right standing with Him—not for my earning it, [but] for His name's sake.

Yes, though I walk through the [deep, sunless] valley of the shadow of death, I will fear or dread no evil, for You are with me; Your rod [to protect] and Your staff [to guide], they comfort me."

She has chosen to walk in gratitude. She wishes it would be over but recognises that it isn't. She understands she's in a fight and instead of letting herself crumble in fear, frustration or fatigue she has found that place and has verbalised that gratitude that I spoke of earlier. Through this attitude of gratitude, she has found hope, strength and the determination she needs to make it through this season of her life.

> *Our children need to be taught gratitude.*

It doesn't come naturally to most, so don't get angry when they don't display gratitude; just teach them. One beautiful way to teach them can be to have a time around the dinner table when everyone, including yourself, shares something they are grateful for in their day or their week. When they hear you being grateful for small things as well as the big things, they will catch it from you. It is a wonderful thing to let them know how you are grateful for qualities within them too.

Write the list out and put it up on display for all to see and ask if they can add to it through the week. Then at the end of the week read them all out and celebrate together.

Where Does The Road Of Gratitude Take Us?

Over the course of the last few years, there has been a lot of conversations around gratitude and the importance of looking closely at our lives and finding what we are grateful for. Many books about gratitude have found their way to Best Seller lists including author, Ann Voskamp's book *One Thousand Gifts* which landed on the *New York Times* Bestseller list for 60 weeks. Her book obviously struck a chord and resonated with many people across the globe. The book is a celebration of grace and recognition of the power of gratitude.

Being grateful holds power beyond what we can even imagine. And, although gratitude has been around for as long as humanity has roamed the planet, it is only the last five years or so that we have realised that gratitude can change our lives. The feeling of gratitude or of being grateful has quickly become the emotion that we measure and we use to pull us out of doom and gloom and catapult us into a new way of being.

It's easy to get lost in a world of being ungrateful. Life has a way of pulling us down; bills need to be paid, family relationships to manage, work demands to juggle, and the list goes on. There is so much that can swallow us up and make us feel like we are drowning. This is when gratitude steps in and helps.

Here are ten ways gratitude can affect us:

1. Happiness – Gratitude makes us happy. When we practice gratitude, we become happier.
2. Satisfaction – Gratitude makes us more satisfied with life. It's not just a fleeting thought; it helps us focus on what we have rather than being distraught by what we don't have.
3. Motivation – Gratitude helps us extend ourselves to others simply by being thankful for what they do or who they are in our lives. A simple thankyou goes a long way and can, in fact, motivate those we are thankful to, to extend themselves and be more in the world.
4. Consumerism – Gratitude can help combat consumerism. By being grateful for what we have and placing value on it, we no longer really 'need' or desire more. Again, satisfaction takes its place.
5. Self-control – Gratitude helps us with self-control simply because we have calmed down and relaxed, we find it easier to apply self-control in our lives.
6. Enrich our children – Displaying gratitude in our homes helps our children because they see gratitude in action. It helps them become more cooperative, have a purpose in life and experience happiness themselves.
7. Improve your relationship – When gratitude is invested in relationships, people have a greater level of intimacy, friendship and mutual respect.
8. Builds social ties – Gratitude helps relationships beyond the personal and intimate. Showing gratitude in other relationships only enhances your life.
9. Better health – Although not fully documented, gratitude has been linked to better sleep habits, stress levels and overall health and well-being.
10. Resilience – When faced with challenges, people who live from a place of gratitude experience more resilience.

> *Gratitude can change us and propel us forward.*

So, whatever you are facing today, whatever life may look like, can I encourage you to embrace gratitude? **Gratitude can change us and propel us forward.** In fact, as I look over the ten points above, I think that by living out of a place of gratitude we will all be happier, healthier and so we become a more powerful person on the planet, impacting the lives of those around us.

Gratitude is powerful.

Fear

When anxiety was great within me,
your consolation brought joy to my
soul.

Psalm 94:19

I Conquered The Mountain

Well, I did it! I wasn't sure how I would go, however I climbed Table Mountain in Cape Town. And, to be clear, Table Mountain is 1085m high. I admit I'm pretty proud of myself for doing this.

When we arrived in Cape Town I saw the imposing mountain towering over us all. It was so high it made everything around it look small and almost insignificant. As I stared at the mountain, I actually felt my stomach tremble with intimidation. I wasn't sure if I had bitten off more than I could possibly chew when it came to hiking up the steep slopes and the more I looked at the vastness of it, the worse I felt.

It was huge, and from my vantage point, it looked like it boasted huge sandstone cliffs wherever you looked. How on God's green earth was I going to climb this mountain? I had seen pictures in brochures, I'd done my research online, but neither the print or digital version gave the intimidating view that I was experiencing in person. At home, in the comfort of my lounge room when I booked this hiking tour, I think I was naïve; what was I thinking, booking a hiking tour TO THE TOP OF THIS ROCK?!

You know how it is, we all feel very brave sitting in our lounge rooms with all our familiar comforts around as we click with confidence and pay with pride. Now I was confronted with reality and I think I was slightly paralysed. I was the only one of our group who was climbing the mountain. We were staying at a hotel at the base and each time I looked out the window there it was staring down at me; Table Mountain in all her splendour. I have to be completely honest, there were times when I looked out that window and looked over at Rob and admitted that I wasn't sure I could do this hike. That being said, with a little fear as my companion, I really wanted to give it my best and at least have a good old Aussie crack at it.

We arrived on Friday and I was booked to climb on Monday. I had the weekend to stare at its compromising stature, allowing the mountain to intimidate me and cause me to consider my options. Before leaving for our South African adventure, I had been dedicated to my usual fitness routine in order to prepare for this hike but for whatever reason, I didn't have time to do the extra work that would have been so beneficial.

We left Sydney for South Africa nearly two weeks before my climb which meant, due to our travel schedule, I didn't have those two weeks of training up my sleeve which contributed to my lack of confidence. Thankfully, our skilled tour guide told me that she would put me to the test in the first 20 minutes of the climb to assess whether she thought I would be able to complete the climb. If I failed her test, she would turn me around and send me back to the safety of our hotel room. I was feeling a little unsure of the whole thing. My ability to complete the hike, to conquer this mountain, was definitely in question.

I decided to look at the situation this way: **I had nothing to lose except pride** and the satisfaction of completing the climb coupled with the money I had paid for the climb; and so my determination to give it a go started to grow.

I went to bed Sunday night with everything laid out ready. My backpack was packed, my hiking clothes were ready to put on first thing and the alarm set to wake me at 5 am. After a light breakfast of fruit, muesli and yoghurt, the 6 am departure time was upon me. I waved goodbye to Rob and set out with my guide. My goal was to do my best at conquering that mountain.

Now, I can say that I'm glad I found my resolve to push through my fears. It is an experience I will NEVER forget for as long as I live. I had a lovely young couple from England join me and before we began, we stood at the bottom and our guide pointed out the track we were about to venture upon. Looking up at the mountain and seeing where we were going to walk made my heart race. What kept me focused was knowing how disappointed I would be (in myself) if I didn't at least attempt this adventure. So, with my fear, concern and determination we set off and began the hike. Important to note: there are over 100 tracks over the mountain and our guide chose to take us on one that took us up the back of the mountain. You can imagine my relief when after 20 minutes she said she was confident I could make it.

As you climb, there are a few short breaks of flat walking in between varying degrees of difficulty; it was amazing. The beautiful vegetation all around reminded me so much of our plants in Australia. Leisel, our guide, was just lovely and so knowledgeable about all the plant and bird life we came across on the track. It took my breath away. The sheer beauty and majesty of it all; the way the plants were created to survive such harsh conditions and the delicate flowers that seemed to smile at me and encourage me up the mountain. We saw so many **magnificent views that are not accessible unless you make the effort to climb the track.** I am not going to deny it, it was hard work and in the last hour my body was crying out to me each time I had to climb another big rock and hang on to scamper up a steep section, however, the rewards were more than worth it. The young couple who was finding it as hard as me, also encouraged me to keep going without doubting myself.

We saw the waterfalls, the towns way down low on the coastline beneath us, the track behind us, the mountains around us, the wildflowers, the dams, the beautiful delicate birds and the magnificent eagles gliding in the sky around us, I couldn't help but be in awe. It took 4:15 hours from the bottom to the top and then 20 minutes to walk over the top to the cable car which would take us down to the waiting car that we had left about four hours earlier.

Rob met us at the top and he had a big smile of relief on his face when he saw that I had made it safely. I am so glad I didn't let pride, fear, intimidation or anything else step in my way and stop me, even though it was tempting every step of the way. As I looked at what seemed impossible from the bottom looking up, I realised that it was all possible, but it required effort from me.

Isn't that just like life? So many times it seems easier to stay in our comfort zone and not step out and up when a challenge comes along or a dream comes to us. I love to tell my precious grandchildren about my adventure and how I wasn't sure I could do this but found the courage and was able to conquer my deepest fears.

The feeling of standing on the top of that mountain with a very tired body knowing there was no more climbing to do, that it was all behind me, was the most amazing, fabulous and exhilarating feeling. At 67 years old I am so excited about being healthy enough to accomplish a hike like this. I can't wait to do another one that will challenge me and give me the same satisfaction. I want my grandchildren to hear stories from their grandmother about how she overcame her fears, all in an effort to help them see and know not to let anything or anyone stop them from following their dreams.

As I reflect on my exhilarating climb up Table Mountain in Cape Town, I can't forget a very profound sentence that our guide said to us. We were sitting on a stone ledge probably about two-thirds of the way up the mountain enjoying the magnificent view as we looked down over a beautiful seaside town way below us. Leisel said that no one can see this magnificent view unless they hike the track. You have to extend yourself and take the risk to be in the right position to see the views we were seeing.

Many people have the opportunity to see truly glorious views when they catch the cable cars up and down this truly imposing mountain and as they walk the paths along the top. You can be truly blessed, see amazing views and be in awe of the majesty of it all; the beautiful city below, the mountains all around, the beaches below, the animal life and the plants at the top. But, by hiking the track we see all of that PLUS so much more. In order to see all of the extra things you must **walk the tracks that much fewer people walk.**

I have learnt in life that this is true. In my experience, if we want to see and achieve beyond our limitations and beyond the norm, we have to walk the tracks that few people walk. It can seem lonely sometimes, there is always a higher price to pay and a lot more effort involved, however the views you see on the way are so worth it.

Never worry if you are the only one out there going the extra mile. **Sometimes life requires us to walk on our own,** daring us to go it alone and even in another direction than the majority. I think the key to this is to know what you want to see and experience in life and do whatever it costs to walk that journey.

As parents and grandparents, we need to encourage our children to not be afraid to go against the crowd; to be like a salmon and 'swim upstream'. To be confident in themselves when they recognise the need to be different and to follow the path they need to walk so that they can see the views they want to see in their lives. We know there are beautiful views in this life that most see and fully enjoy, but **let's not miss out on the other** *extraordinary* *views* that are there for us all to see when we extend ourselves and walk the path that few are brave enough to walk.

What a magnificent world we live in. I am believing Psalm 92:14 that promises that in my old age I will be flourishing. Let's create stories we can share with the young children in our lives so that they can dream big and become overcomers themselves.

As you will learn in the next chapter, we have help to enable us to walk unusual paths to see the ***extraordinary*** views.

Angels In Our Midst

Have you ever been scared of anything? Have you ever woken to the screams of a child who has had a scary dream? Or maybe fear has crept in through a television show, movie or even a story book.

Fear has a way of sneaking into our hearts and minds in unique and unexpected ways and sometimes, when fear has found its way in, it's difficult to get rid of that fear. It's an interesting emotion, *Psychology Today* says:

> Fear is generally considered a reaction to something immediate that threatens your security or safety, such as being startled by someone suddenly jumping out at you from behind a bush. The emotion of fear is felt as a sense of dread, alerting you to the possibility that your physical self might be harmed, which in turn motivates you to protect yourself.

As parents, the emotion of fear is definitely a tough one to navigate and teach our children about. How do we explain that what we are feeling is about something that might or might not happen? The complexities of fear are astounding.

Today, I would love to share with you, a conversation I recently had with my gorgeous granddaughter, Mia. Mia, who was three years old at the time, was going through a stage when she was frightened throughout the day but especially at night. The dark always adds a new dimension and element to fear. Mia was frightened that something or someone was going to get her and hurt her (as mentioned above, a sense of dread). Mia's feelings were compounded by the fact that her five-year-old brother, Joshua, had a fascination with running around the house being a scary monster or a witch or anything he thinks would be scary. He liked to tell Mia that, "I'm going to get you." Needless to say, this situation wasn't helping Mia.

This is something Mia had to walk through and as tough as it was, it's important that she learned how to feel and to understand that she was safe, no matter what. Mia's mother, Leanne (my daughter-in-love) and her father (my lovely son) were trying their best to teach Josh not to scare his sister. They explained that it isn't nice to make someone feel scared and although he found it amusing, what she's feeling was very real and was unsettling for her.

Although Josh needed to be taught this valuable lesson, what was more empowering for Mia, was that her parents were teaching her why she didn't need to feel scared. They were teaching Mia that she could be confident knowing she was safe from all those scary things like monsters, witches or anything else because angels are looking after her all the time. Leanne was teaching Mia at a young age how to use the thought and understanding of angels for protection. She has told Mia that she can speak to her angels and ask them to stand at each corner of their property so nothing bad can enter their house.

> *The thought and understanding of angels is something that children relate to well.*

Angels have this ethereal, heavenly quality about them that provide this beautiful sense of peace.

As I've been thinking about this and remembering the chats with Mia about her fears, I'm reminded of one of my favourite verses in the bible. It's Psalm 91:9-12 which shows us that we all have angels that are created to protect us and they will hold us up with their hands so we won't be hurt. What a beautiful thought and picture that is painted for us to hold on to.

"God, you're my refuge. I trust in you and I'm safe!" That's right— he rescues you from hidden traps, shields you from deadly hazards. His huge outstretched arms protect you— under them you're perfectly safe; his arms fend off all harm. Fear nothing—not wild wolves in the night, not flying arrows in the day, not disease that prowls through the darkness, not disaster that erupts at high noon. Even though others succumb all around, drop like flies right and left, no harm will even graze you. You'll stand untouched, watch it all from a distance, and watch the wicked turn into corpses. Yes, because God's your refuge, the High God your very own home, Evil can't get close to you, harm can't get through the door. He ordered his angels to guard you wherever you go. If you stumble, they'll catch you; their job is to keep you from falling."

As a grandmother, it is wonderful to confidently reassure Mia that she can ask the angels to be with her wherever she is, and she can be sure they are big and strong. I tell her that some even have swords that will deal with anything at all for her. They are like Heavenly Superheroes that we have access to. I tell her that I think there are a lot of bored angels out there because we aren't calling out for their help and we aren't assigning them duty over us and our families. So together, we called on an angel to be by Mia's side.

Personally, I believe we all have angels that have been especially assigned to us. We just need to call on them and ask them to walk with us, protecting us, warning us and loving us.

When Mia heard the truth about angels, she was one very happy little girl. She is now walking in the knowledge that she has a strong angel looking out for her. I can see her little eyes light up when she thinks or talks about her strong angel and I can tell that she is much more confident and able to deal with her fears.

I love knowing that Mia understands that she is protected and that Rob and I and our family are safe under the protection of strong angels that are commanded over us.

By the way, Josh is a work in progress; being a little boy he loves to scare whomever he can... Boys, you have to love them!

Taking Stock

> The path of development is a journey of discovery that is clear only in retrospect, and it's rarely a straight line.
>
> **Eileen Kennedy-Moore**

An Interview With My Children

As parents it is our desire for things to go well with our children and for them to have a full and long life. We as parents, I believe, hold the key in our hands to unlock this for them.

Often the pressure is put on children to honour their mother and father. I believe as parents we have the huge privilege of equipping our children to be able to do this and to reap the promise that it brings. Clearly none of us have perfect parenting skills. We all have our strengths and weaknesses. Knowing this, I decided to sit down with my own adult children and ask them what they thought I had done well. In other words, I asked them what I had done to empower them to honour their parents. I also asked them to tell me what they thought my weaknesses as a parent had been.

I felt quite vulnerable doing this, but my advice to you is to **never be afraid of being vulnerable in front of your children** because the rewards are worth it. They benefit so much seeing you unafraid of being vulnerable and willing to see things from their perspective and being open to change for the sake of your relationship with them, which you value more than anything else.

So, I would like to firstly share with you what my children said I had done well.

1. **A strong relationship between Rob and myself.**
    This gives your children stability and confidence in you, themselves and the world they live in. It helps them to be strong in their own identity and helps them be able to make strong,

healthy attachments for themselves. When we show our children that we honour and value each other they learn how to honour and value us and others. We need to be deliberate about adding value to our partner. We cannot put our children first before our spouse or partner. There are of course times when our children need our attention more than our partner, but overall, we need to show our children just how important we are to each other. Even if you separate you can show this to your children. All is not lost. You can still show their father or mother respect and add value to them and in doing so you add value to your children.

2. Unconditional Love

In a nutshell, this is the kind of love my children were talking about:

They need to know there is no pressure to be anything or anyone else other than who they are and who they are becoming. They can always be more than confident that they will receive love from us purely and simply because they are our children and they are a part of us. We don't give them love because of anything they do or anything they achieve.

There is no condemnation in this love. There are consequences but NO condemnation. Condemnation only brings shame and blame and closes the child down. We must never disapprove of our child or be ashamed of them being our child. We can disapprove of some of the choices they make and of their behaviour at times, but we can learn to do this without demeaning or devaluing them in any way. **They need to know without a doubt that they still mean the world to us regardless of their choices.**

3. **Rob and I always believe IN them**

   Our children said they always know that Rob and I believe in them.

   When we believe in them they learn to believe in themselves. Rob and I always reminded our children that they are 'God's masterpiece'. There is pure gold in each of your children. Sometimes you only find gold by digging in the dirt to find it. You may have to dig deep at times and you may have to get your hands dirty, but there is a treasure of high quality gold in each and every one. Don't be afraid of the dirt; don't let the mistakes they make side track you and don't give up on them.

   Do your children know that you believe in them because of what you say to them and about them and by the way you encourage their dreams and support them in those dreams? If we believe in them, they will believe in themselves and know how to take risks when necessary to become all they were created to be.

4. **Giving them time**

   Give them your time and make them your priority above other people and things. I have given ideas on how to give them your time in previous chapters, so I won't repeat them here.

5. **Major on the majors**

   Your Family Code of Conduct will guide you in this. If a family code of conduct has been or will be broken, then that is a Major and requires attention or requires your 'No'. If not, then it's a Minor. I remember getting disapproving looks from fellow parents one day when I bleached two of my sons' hair and coloured one blue and one bright green. It was important for them to have their hair done this way and even though I didn't understand why it was, I made it important to me despite the disapproval from some of my peers. I made sure it was done in the school holidays to show them they needed to respect school uniform code, however, by allowing them to express themselves like this I showed them that they meant more to me than other people's opinions of me.

Don't hold grudges or be moody with your children when you need to discipline them because they have stepped outside of the Family Code of Conduct.

Make your discipline reasonable and never hold onto anger or be manipulative by being cold towards them afterwards. Forgive and let go and don't let the sun go down on your anger. Let them know **your love for them doesn't depend on their behaviour** and that they will always be loved by you no matter what.

6. My value and belief system

I live this out in front of them. They will catch much more than they are taught. I didn't just talk about it and I didn't leave it to others.

I listened to their faith journey.

I tried not to rely on my own wisdom for parenting but asked God for wisdom. It has helped me tremendously.

I pray for my children regularly and teach them to pray – never underestimate their most simple of prayers. It gives my children and grandchildren a lot of confidence just knowing that I pray for them daily.

Now let me share with you the thing my children said I was weak on:

I didn't sit with them enough in their pain. They said I was too ready with answers that worked for me instead of looking for answers that would work for them or waiting with them while they discovered the answers for themselves.

Because I am a very positive person and don't dwell too long on negative things and like to move forward and find solutions to problems I tend to move past pain too quickly. Sometimes your children need you to just listen and let them process the challenges they come up against in their lives. They just need you to sit with them and wait for them to find the answers. Sometimes that takes a lot longer than expected, but it's worth waiting with them for.

Final Encouragement

I want to leave you with a very important message that I would love all of you young parents to take on board for yourselves so that you have the freedom to enjoy your parenting.

> *You don't have to parent your children perfectly to parent them well.*

Don't put yourself or your children under the pressure of never making a mistake in your parenting. Your children don't need perfect parents, they only need parents who love them unconditionally, who believe in them completely and who are aware of their own limitations whilst attempting to do their best.

Perfectionism will eat you up and destroy your relationship with your children because you will always have a feeling of failure hanging over you as the parent and your children will feel pressured to be perfect in order to receive love and approval from you. It's amazing how grace for yourself releases grace into your children and gives you both the space to enjoy each other. If you have regrets about your parenting in the past, no matter if you have older children like me or whatever age they are, it is never too late. It's never too late to apologise, be vulnerable and to grow as a parent; you have done your best and all of us can improve on our best as we learn more.

Go, have fun, enjoy your parenting and raise those precious champions you have been blessed to call your children.

Susanna Bateman
Author Profile

Author and facilitator of early childhood learning, development and high-quality care

Susanna Bateman, along with her husband Rob, are the co-founders of Little Miracles, a chain of nine early education and long day care centres. Little Miracles focuses on developing children's literacy skills through fun activities in a nurturing environment. Susanna and Rob have both been blessed by their Christian faith and seek to incorporate Christian principles in all their endeavours.

Susanna's goal to encourage a lifelong love of reading and learning among the children in Little Miracles' care is inspired by her own personal experiences. By the time she left school, Susanna had never completely read a book. She was dyslexic, only managing to overcome her reading difficulty when she was an adult.

Susanna and Rob also helped their own four children beat dyslexia. Now adults themselves, they work with Susanna and Rob at Little Miracles and between them have produced twelve grandchildren.

Besides their passion for early childhood learning and development, Rob and Susanna also like to travel. They have been to countries, cities and regions all over the world including New Zealand, Canada, the USA,

Hong Kong, the Caribbean, Paris, India, London, Ireland, Rwanda, South Africa, Venice, Indonesia, Switzerland and Fiji. They have also given back to the community through dedicating their time to worthy causes.

Susanna has been a volunteer youth leader for fifteen years. She has spent time working with parents to prevent child abuse as well as mentoring young mothers. She has also spoken at Christian women's conferences. Susanna is the author of *Enjoy Your Parenting* and lives in New South Wales, Australia with her family.

Recommended
resources

Little Miracles
Loving Children • Growing Champions

Together Rob and Susanna founded Little Miracles Childcare Centres.

For many years Susanna was heavily involved in community work with children, youth and women. Together Rob and Susanna have always been passionate about helping families and making a difference in people's lives.

They both love children, with four of their own and twelve beautiful grandchildren.

Their four children experienced dyslexia at a young age and they found that there weren't many facilities available that helped in this area. Childcare centers were literally no more than that – child*care*. And kindergartens were simply just a progression of a childcare center.

This led to a big question that in Rob's opinion was the missing gap in the industry…

How can a childcare center also improve a child's overall learning ability, ideally taking place during the growth phases of any child, while allowing them to play, grow, and explore their own world freely at their own pace?

Before deciding to start their own childcare center, they saw the critical importance of encouraging children to become all they were designed to be. They believe that a child's pre-school years are one of the most important stages of their life.

Rob and Susanna wanted to add value to children's lives.

Over the past 15 years, they have improved and evolved their system in their centers, developing an outstanding team that is now able to provide one of the highest quality child care programs available in the industry today.

Little Miracles are proud to consistently win awards for their childcare centres. Most recently they have been declared the National Winners Australian Achiever Awards for excellence in customer service five years in a row!

There are currently nine Little Miracles Centres with one more planned for later in 2019, located in the Blue Mountains, the Central Coast of New South Wales and Newcastle.

For more information you can visit their website at:

www.LittleMiracles.com.au

Susan Sohn and GetRealLive

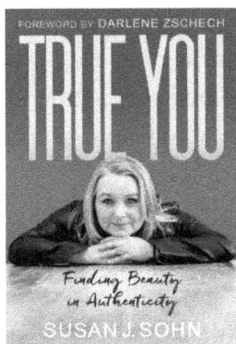

Susan J. Sohn is a community builder, speaker, writer, retreat facilitator, and online/social media entrepreneur. She is best described as raw, honest, disarming, and immediately relatable. Susan has the ability to gather people and create rich community. Her table is a place where everyone is welcome, everyone has a voice, and everyone is heard. Her lifestyle business GetRealLive has been built with love and wisdom has spawned a successful marketing business SOMO Society and they regularly run retreats.

The GetRealLive Retreat is a time to gather, to connect, and to leave ready to live the life you dream of living. These are designed with you in mind. Every moment is intentionally crafted for you to walk through and into something new. From the moment you register, our goal and desire is to treat you, to challenge you, and to ignite your senses and help you take the next brave step. Visit the retreat page on Susan's website to see some of the incredible photos, videos, and stories of those who have taken part in one of our retreats.

Susan's first book, True You: Finding Beauty in Authenticity was released in early December 2018. Find the true you and lead a life of authenticity. This insightful book encourages you to;

- reject the harmful lies society tells you and the lies you've told yourself
- embrace pain and vulnerability as you learn to walk in truth
- Connect and celebrate with women on the same journey to authenticity.
- Get out of your own way and allow freedom to become reality.
- Know who you are in God

Website: https://getreallive.com

Mini Me Bee

Special Offer

Offering you 25% off all of our toys

Hi I'm Emily, I am a speech pathologist and I have loved helping children communicate for the last decade

Over my time as a speech pathologist, I have seen that children learn best when learning is fun, engaging and interesting. Toys are a must for learning!

Mini Me Bee brings to all children, worldwide, and parents; educational products of the highest industry standards.

I hope that your children and you love our products, like we do! Please get to know Mini Me Bee first hand on our facebook page and Instagram, @MiniMeBee

Be sure to share with us your favourite products! #minimebee

To claim this special offer, enter this code at checkout: **MIRACLE25**

www.minimebee.com